To: Daniel
From: Dad.
Xmas 1984.
( 2nd time round!)

# Cricket: Umpiring

SPORTING SKILLS SERIES

# Cricket: Umpiring

## DAVID CONSTANT

### WITH THE ASSISTANCE OF PATRICK MURPHY

PELHAM BOOKS

First published in Great Britain by
PELHAM BOOKS LTD
44 Bedford Square
London WC1B 3DU
1981

The photographs are reproduced by courtesy of the
following: Patrick Eagar (on pages 14, 15 *below,* 16, 31,
38, 39, 41 *below,* 47, 48, 56, 58, 59, 60, 61, 68, 71, 73, 82,
83 *left,* 101, 102, 110, 111); Ken Kelly (on pages 15 *above,*
17, 19, 22, 27, 36, 41 *above,* 44-5, 83 *right,* 106-7, 112, 113,
114, 115) and News Ltd, Sydney (on page 43)

ISBN 0 7207 1302 1

Typeset in Great Britain by
Cambrian Typesetters, Farnborough, Hants
Printed and bound in Singapore

# Contents

Umpiring is more than just a job to David Constant. After reading only a few pages of this entertaining book, it is abundantly obvious that he has the game in his blood and could never happily be very far away from it. So it was cricket's lucky day when Leicestershire gave him the sack as a young player. All the enthusiasm that would have gone into mere batting and fielding was suddenly available in a different form. Here was a young man who was not just taking to umpiring as a kind of occupational pension, but as a full-time career.

Because he had a less illustrious playing record than most of the others on the first-class list, he had something to prove from the moment he donned a white coat. He simply had to be better at the job than the others or nobody would have taken him seriously. So he set about the job seriously and made it to the top in double-quick time. Soon he had the status to ensure automatic selection to stand in Tests and that is where the fun really started for him.

This is what gives the book a sharply topical flavour. His opinions of modern players are bang up-to-date, keenly observed at close quarters and, like his decisions on the field, have a deliberate impartiality which gives weight to what he says.

As I have often thought about umpires — and captains too, come to that — it is less important actually to be right than for all the players to think you are right. To this extent umpiring is not so much a matter of mathematical accuracy as an exercise in leadership which enormously extends the scope of the job for the right kind of man. So it is not surprising to find that Constant has been chairman of the first-class umpires.

He is an established leader, and what he has to say about the game's problems is worth reading. On the question of discipline, for instance, it is reassuring to know that he and other Test umpires are already playing quite a vigorous role in keeping the occasional rough diamond in his place. Constant even advocates short periods of suspension for flagrant offenders — rather on the sin-bin ice-hockey principle — which would add spice to the game if nothing else.

What Mr Constant has successfully achieved in committing his life and times to paper is to awaken in this reader a greater awareness of the indispensable service to the game which umpires provide. That cricket can attract people of such quality to undertake what is a desperately difficult assignment is a compliment in itself. That it has been fortunate enough to gain the services of David Constant is a windfall of significant proportions.

TED DEXTER
April 1980

# 1 What Makes an Umpire?

The short answer to that question is: 'The wisdom of a 90-year-old in the body of an 18-year-old.' Seriously, though, the qualities needed by a good umpire at any level of cricket are a combination of physical abilities, mental toughness and common sense.

Don't let anyone tell you umpires aren't *that* important in a game of cricket. Bad umpiring can be soul-destroying. I wonder how many young cricketers are put off the game by a series of bad decisions from an incompetent umpire? At first-class level the players expect, and are entitled to, good umpires — but at club or school level the standards are very erratic. Many village sides who wouldn't dream of playing with ten men are quite happy to enlist somebody to umpire on the spot when they arrive at a match — yet a few howlers by that willing umpire can ruin a match.

I can really feel for club cricketers who suffer bad umpiring. During the week the club player turns up at the nets and helps out his team in all the usual off-field activities like watering the wicket or sorting out the club's finances. Then at the weekend he's given out, caught at the wicket, when his bat was about three feet from the ball. It's the same for a bowler who gets a man out plumb, even to the extent that the batsman's already leaving the crease, only for the half-awake umpire to say, 'Not out'. Schoolboy cricketers have the same problems — often the umpire is a teacher or classmate who doesn't really understand the game or care about the consequences of bad decisions.

It really helps if the umpire in any class of cricket has played the game himself. It doesn't matter if he was just a mediocre trundler with the ball or a batsman who barely managed to stay at the wicket for ten minutes, but if he has managed to absorb the ethics and the basics of the game he should be able to umpire. He should know the little tricks of the trade, the players who try to con the umpire and the scrupulously fair bowlers or wicket-keepers who won't waste the umpire's time by unnecessary appeals. If he's played the game for a few years, the umpire should be able to withstand intimidation from the fielding side and to judge instinctively from the batsman's reaction that he realizes he's touched a delivery.

My theory is: 'The lesser the player, the better the umpire.' The chap who's got bags of ability isn't normally a deep thinker on the game, whereas the mediocre player has to work and concentrate to compensate for his lack of natural ability. That theory applies to first-class cricket in particular. I can't think of many first-class umpires in my time who were quality cricketers as well. Arthur Fagg and John Langridge were fine players, and so were Ken Palmer and Peter Wight, but the bulk of them were average cricketers who had to rely on something other than sheer class to stay in the game.

The latter category certainly included me. I played for Kent and Leicestershire for eight seasons in the 1960s and I managed the grand total of 1,500 runs at an average of 20. It's fair to say that the game gave *me* up, rather than the other way round — bowlers up and down the country convinced me I had no future in top-class cricket as a player. I performed well enough in the Second XI for Kent, becoming the first batsman ever to get 1,000 runs for them in one season, but with people like Mike Denness, Brian Luckhurst and Bob Woolmer in the side competition was fierce among the youngsters. Things didn't really improve when I tried my luck with Leicestershire, and the crunch came when I was left out of a Gillette Cup quarter-final tie at Lord's. I felt I should have played, but my exclusion meant that my county didn't really think I was up to it. That was confirmed by the county's secretary, Mike Turner, so I decided to think of ways of staying in the game that I loved. I was only 27, without any prospects as a player, and with no administrative experience, so what could I do?

Enter Dave Halfyard, one of the men who helped shape my umpiring career. I'd known Dave for years and he'd already had a stint on the umpires' list before returning to the game as a medium-pace bowler with Nottinghamshire. Dave was staying with me in my house at Leicester at the time of my personal crisis and he said, 'Why not apply for the umpires' list?' I'd never thought of that, and on reflection it was indeed one way of staying in cricket. I filled in the appropriate form, Mike Turner recommended me to Lord's, and in the winter of 1968 (without even an exam or an interview) I was told I'd been appointed a first-class umpire. Obviously the powers-that-be assumed that a former county player knew enough about the laws of the game and the way it's played, so I didn't have to go through many formalities. But I had to do some swotting-up before my début in May 1969. *Wisden* devoted 36 pages to the laws and I soon realized how much a county player doesn't know about the small print. My wife Rosalyn used to sit up in bed at night quizzing me about the laws, and sometimes I thought my brain would burst with all the sub-sections and minor details. . . .

So at the age of twenty-eight years and six months I stood in my first match — a John Player League game at Chelmsford between Essex and Nottinghamshire. Early on, Gary Sobers was run out for 0 (not my decision) and then came my first not out. Ray East, the Essex left-arm spinner, bowled one that was going down the leg side. It hit the batsman's pad and all the close fielders and the bowler went up in a loud appeal. When I turned it down they all smiled, so I can only assume they were just testing the water a little!

My biggest fear at the start was whether the players would accept decisions from a young man who wasn't all that good a cricketer. I'd imagined things like, 'How can we take that new bloke Constant seriously? He was never all that good as a batsman.' Luckily, first-class cricketers aren't like that. They accept you for the way you are and how you react to circumstances, rather than judge you on the amount of caps you've won. It was difficult to adjust to being an umpire just seven months after I'd been playing with and against most of the blokes around the counties. So I concentrated like mad at the start and tried hard to avoid starting up conversations on the field of play with old mates. I suppose I appeared rather remote at that time because of my need to concentrate on every delivery and appear in control of the situation. I'd worry initially about my progress but gradually I started picking up encouraging noises from the players. I remember Merv Kitchen, a good friend from the Somerset side, saying to me early in my first season, 'Well done, I hear you're doing quite well.' That meant a lot to me and I settled down.

I was lucky in that I started umpiring in the days when batsmen still walked if they'd touched the ball. I was brought up in the old school that tried to make things easy for the umpire — if you knew you were out, you'd tuck the bat under your arm and be off before the umpire's finger came up. In 1969 90 per cent of the batsmen were walkers, and sometimes I'd think to myself, 'Good job he walked, otherwise I wouldn't have given him out.' Having the co-operation of the players in that respect helped me build up my confidence in those early months.

It could be frustrating as well, though. I'd find myself thinking, 'They never bowled those full tosses and half volleys at me when I was a batsman,' but I suppose that was wishful thinking. I'm still wistful about not making the grade as a player, and when I see blokes like Arnold Long, Keith Fletcher, Norman Gifford and Derek Underwood still playing, I get nostalgic. I came up through county cricket with these lads and I wish I'd made the grade like them. Although I'm still involved in the game and love my job, nothing can compare with the fun and comradeship of being one player in a team. You live with your team-mates, travel the country, share a few pints, laughs and heartbreaks — and it's like losing an arm when it's all over. An umpire, on the other hand, mustn't be too friendly, too ready with the banter. In my first few seasons wearing a white coat I had to learn to stifle a smile when someone said something funny on the field of play. I've learned to relax my guard now, but an umpire must always avoid over-familiarity with the players, otherwise his authority will gradually be eroded.

I had to get used to other things in my early days as an umpire — like back-ache. Because I wanted to concentrate so fiercely, I was always down beside the stumps as the bowler delivered; but the strain was too much and I settled for leaning forward from an upright position. There were embarrassing moments at the start — in my first few matches I'd find myself walking in from square leg as the bowler ran up! If there was a chance of a run-out when I stood at the bowler's end, I used to back up as though I was still a fielder, rather than position myself as an umpire. It was very difficult to forget the habits of a cricketer in such a short space of time, but I got them out of my system after a few matches.

By far the biggest strain was the mental one; because of my fears about being too young and inexperienced, I concentrated very hard in my first two seasons. I kept a note of all the wicket-keeper's catches I'd given (37 in 1969, 33 the following season), just to see if things evened themselves out over a period of time. But I was shattered at close of play, far more mentally tired than in my playing days. I realized that, no matter how unobtrusive the umpire, he's a tired man at close of play if he's doing his job properly.

So what makes a good umpire? Try this lot for a start — good eyesight and hearing; a thick skin and good temper; integrity; a judicial mind; a good, strong pair of legs; physical fitness; the ability to concentrate for long periods; a working knowledge of the laws and consistency in applying them in the spirit of the game; and a philosophical frame of mind that stops you taking

12

your problems home with you. Now that's not a lot, is it? Much of the task is about common sense and a belief in your own ability to do a difficult job, but if I had to choose the most valuable asset it would be the ability to concentrate for long periods.

In my experience the transition from player to umpire isn't massive if you've been a batsman, a wicket-keeper or a specialist close fielder. These men are used to concentrating throughout the day, unlike a bowler who can graze contentedly down at third man during and after his stint. Many of the top umpires have been ideally suited from a mental point of view by their early cricketing careers — John Langridge was a slip/batsman, Charlie Elliott a batsman, Sid Buller a keeper, Arthur Fagg and Harold Bird were batsmen. As I was a short-leg fielder and loosely described as a batsman, I also had a head start when it came to concentrating, although I didn't usually stay at the crease for many hours when I batted for Kent and Leicestershire!

As an umpire, you've got to sustain a high level of concentration for longer periods than a player. In the one-day games that form a large part of English cricket an umpire has to be on his toes every ball because something's always likely to happen — a quick, scrambled single here and a desperate slog there. And it's a long day in the Gillette or Benson and Hedges competitions, with over 100 overs likely to be bowled, compared with 80 on a normal Test match day. And if there's rain about, you've got to get your pocket calculator out and check periodically what time remains. In the old days there were simply Tests, county matches and games involving the touring side to worry about; now we have the Gillette, Prudential and Benson and Hedges trophies plus the John Player League. So it's important to remember what day it is when you're donning the white coat in the morning!

From five o'clock onwards you sometimes have to grit your teeth and really knuckle down to the rest of the day's play. And if you're feeling tired your concentration will be impaired. Try

*An umpire needs to be on his toes every ball in case he has to get into the proper side-on position for a run-out at the bowler's end. Lloyd Budd (above), Ray Julian, (right) Dusty Rhodes (opposite above) and Peter Wight (opposite below) have all passed the test with flying colours*

14

*A first-class umpire has to worry about things like the weather as well as the laws of the game. Ken Palmer takes a light reading during the Lord's Test of 1979, while Graham Gooch is in no doubt that he'll soon be putting his feet up in the pavilion.*

to view physical fitness in the same way as a player — do as much training as you can to develop a strong pair of legs. When you're standing in one place for a long time the blood flows to the bottom of your feet, which makes your legs ache. Between overs, I jog up and down on the balls of my feet, trying to keep the muscles moving. If you are worried about your legs, do as much walking as possible in the winter, try leg exercises (in my case, a couple of pounds of sugar on each foot and I raise them 20 times per foot daily), and play golf. If your legs give out on you, your performance as an umpire will be impaired. I've had

*No-balls can be a problem. The umpire has to watch the position of the bowler's front foot and then refocus instantly on where the ball is about to pitch. As Lloyd Budd would surely agree, that's a problem with a fast bowler like Jeff Thomson*

17

varicose vein trouble for a few seasons now and it gave me some pain in my right leg as I stood all day. But an operation's cleared that up.

Every April the first-class umpires undergo a medical which covers eyesight, hearing and blood pressure. I test my hearing with my doctor's help. He keeps a watch with an almost silent tick in the top drawer of his desk, and if I can't hear it I'm in trouble. One year I couldn't manage it and I thought I was going deaf, but a quick syringe job did the trick! The pressure on an umpire's eyesight is considerable — if you're standing at square leg you've got to check the fairness of the bowler's action, then focus the eyes to the stumps at the striker's end, especially if a slow bowler's on and the wicket-keeper is standing up. The same applies if you're at the bowler's end. Although the laws governing the front foot rule mean that the bowler is no longer delivering the ball from just 18 yards, this situation needs extra vigilance from the umpire. He now has less time to look from the bowler's front foot to the wicket where the ball will be pitching. The umpire's reactions must be quick and he must be able to refocus immediately. So if you're worried about your eyesight, wear glasses. Umpires like Arthur Jepson, Alan Whitehead and Tom Spencer are better at their job because they recognize the need to wear glasses. So forget about vanity if you want to be a good umpire.

One thing all you budding umpires should never forget — the man in the white coat doesn't make laws, he simply enforces them. Never get involved in justifying your decisions on the field, because that will undermine your authority. By all means talk about it in the bar afterwards when the offended player's temper may well have been soothed, but at no stage are you under any obligation to give reasons for your actions. Make sure you apply the laws in the spirit of the game. I find a lot of club umpires know the laws of cricket backwards, but because they have little playing experience they tend to apply them literally. This is where common sense helps — there's nothing wrong with a little interpretation where the regulation isn't

OPPOSITE *Common sense is a vital ingredient when umpiring. Some slow bowlers prefer the umpire to stand right up to the stumps to give them an unimpeded run to the wicket, while others would rather the umpire stood back. In both cases, the bowler's wishes should be respected, and there's no need to brandish the big stick. In the photograph on the left New Zealand's Stephen Boock has asked 'Dickie' Bird to stand right up, whereas in the photograph on the right England's Geoff Miller wants me back a little*

18

dogmatic. Make sure of one thing, though — always carry a pocket version of the laws on to the field of play, so that if anybody tries it on you can put him in his place straight away by stopping the game and quoting chapter and verse. Some players love to tease you with little conundrums over a pint — I remember dear old John Mortimore's questions whenever I stood in a match involving his county, Gloucestershire. John, a deep thinker on the game, always had a little brain-teaser ready for me in the umpires' room before the match started. I enjoy things like that because it shows that the English first-class umpire is still respected by the county pro.

Keep mugging up on the laws — they change a little here and there every season — and be consistent in applying them. Players will accept you if you keep giving batsmen out lbw when they sweep, but if you give contradictory decisions from day to day they'll start appealing for everything and then there's a risk that things might go a little sour. Work out your policy about lbws and stick to it as much as possible.

How does an umpire get his hand in before the season starts in earnest? After all, a player can be in the nets all winter, improving his batting technique against the quickies or trying to develop the outswinger, but an umpire can't really do much except keep fit and refresh his memory on the laws. In April I normally stand in a couple of village matches so that I can familiarize myself with the angles, where to stand for a possible run-out, learn to count up to 6 balls an over again — and just regain the feel of standing in the middle. Anything that improves an umpire's performance is worthwhile. Even in the summer, if I want to make sure my angles are right I'll walk over to where the bowler delivered and see where he has to pitch the ball to be able to hit the wicket. That way my mind is programmed before an lbw decision is needed.

At any level of cricket the good umpire stands out for one main reason — he *doesn't* stand out. That's not as Irish as it sounds — the point I'm making is that the umpire, like the soccer or rugby referee, can contribute to the quality of the game by keeping his personality out of the action. Don't be sombre or gloomy. Be serious-minded, but cheerful when necessary. Let the players get on with the game, and if they're happy with you there'll be no real problem.

An umpire always dreads being embarrassed by his decisions, but one way to avoid a certain amount of humiliation is to make sure the essentials of the task are met. Always start on time — it's better to hold up play for a minute than to start a minute late. I had to start a first-class match late when someone forgot to ring the five-minute bell, and I didn't like it, because the game and the players should be respected. Don't forget to mark down who's next to take strike when there's a drinks break. Once, in a Test against Australia, I was caught out and didn't realize it until that evening when Bill Frindall, the BBC's statistical expert, pointed out the error. It happened when Alan Knott and Geoff Boycott staged their famous recovery at Trent Bridge in 1977. Boycott faced up to the next over after drinks, even though he'd taken the previous over! As one wag put it, 'We all know Boycott likes to bat, but that was ridiculous!'

Remember the essentials for the field of play. The counters for every over, a copy of the rules, a spare ball in case the match ball goes out of shape, another bail, a cloth in case rain makes the ball wet, a penknife to cut any loose bits of leather off the ball or to trim anything off a bowler's boot. It all helps if the players believe you're in control of your duties.

Whatever happens during the day's play, don't take your mistakes home with you. If an umpire can sleep soundly, he's done a good job. Even if he's made a mistake but didn't realize it till later, he shouldn't chastise himself too much because an umpire can only give what he sees at that particular time. He doesn't have the advantage of action replay techniques or the gift of second sight, and if he's conscientious and efficient enough he shouldn't search his soul too much after the game's over.

It can be a thankless task. Few people come up to you and say, 'Well umpired,' whereas a cricketer who's performed well that day can be the centre of attraction. Everybody likes to be praised, but an umpire has to stand apart from the back-slapping. He must learn that praise for him comes when people say, 'What'll you have to drink?' or 'Come and meet so-and-so.' The time to worry about your standards is when nobody wants to meet your eye in the clubhouse afterwards — and even then, if you think you did your best and have nothing to regret, try not to let it bother you.

There are compensations, of course. You're still part of the game that you love, even though it *is* second-best if you're no longer a player. My advice to a club cricketer is simple: keep

*An umpire often needs two pairs of eyes. Here Dennis Amiss was within a whisker of being run out when Pakistan's Wasim Baro whipped off the bails. Umpire 'Dickie' Bird had to take in Amiss' bat in relation to the line, to make sure it wasn't in the air but grounded, and also to watch when the wicket was broken by Wasim. Amiss was given 'not out' though 'Dickie' later admitted that the TV action replay showed he was wrong.*

playing as long as you can, but if you still love cricket when you're getting past it, if you would miss the good fellowship and the essential decency of those who play the game, and you dread losing touch with them, don't hesitate — get a copy of the laws and try the white coat on for size. It's better than cutting yourself off from a game that's given you pleasure for more years than you care to remember. And believe me, the joys of cricket are still there for an umpire. Although everyone's just a pair of pads to me when they're at the crease, I still get immense pleasure from seeing the great players at close quarters. It's a thrill to see Derek Randall fielding so superbly, or to stand at square leg and watch the beautifully fluid run-up of Michael Holding. Your legs may be aching, you're wondering why the scorers won't return your signal, and the fast bowler may be giving you the big stare after you've turned down an lbw appeal . . . but I assure you it's better than working for a living!

# 2 Pressures on an Umpire

'Pressure' is very much a modern word. I hear it bandied about all over the place and sometimes I wonder whether too much notice is taken of alleged pressures, especially in sport. I believe people who play sport for a living do it for the fundamental reason that they enjoy it and that it's lovely to be paid as well. In cricket there's a lot of talk about 'the pressures of the modern game', and one would think that they also rub off on the umpire. As far as I'm concerned the umpire makes his own pressures, and I think it's much worse for the players.

I believe that the game is no different for an umpire at the start of the day's play than at the finish when there are 2 wickets left, 20 runs to get and 15 minutes to go. If you get involved in the tensions and start reacting to the pressures the players are feeling, I don't think you're doing your job properly. *Of course* you should worry inwardly whether you're still doing the right things — and I'm not blasé about my performances, I assure you. It's a slur against me if I realize I've done something wrong, and I'll kick myself and curse for the rest of the match. I shan't worry if a batsman was out when I've said so (because I've judged it on the available evidence), but I *will* worry about whether the decision was right — and there's a difference between the two standpoints.

As a player, I was more nervous than as an umpire — perhaps because I'm a better umpire than batsman. A batsman is surely more apprehensive when he's sitting with his pads on, waiting to face up to a couple of quickies in bad light, than an umpire who only has to be called on if a decision is needed. It's up to the player to hit the ball in the middle of the bat, or edge it to the slips; the pressure's on him, not me. And an umpire can make a genuine, regrettable error, yet still be there in the middle at the end of the day, while a player's mistake can affect his whole career.

Some of our English lads have been under certain strains in recent years that umpires never experience. People like John Edrich, Dennis Amiss, Keith Fletcher and Tony Greig faced a barrage of fast stuff at Test level for a long time. There were Lillee, Thomson and Walker one year and Roberts, Holding and Co. the next . . . on wickets of uneven bounce, so the batsmen didn't really know what was coming next. I've stood in many of those matches in the seventies when the ball was flying around all over the place, and nobody can ever tell me that the umpire faces untold pressures compared with the players.

Money has altered the game for the players. I don't think they have the time to enjoy the game in England as much as, say, a decade ago, because after a match they're down the motorway to another fixture with no time to stop, savour the day's play and while away a pleasant, reflective hour or two in the bar. They also have to concentrate on bowling so many overs an hour, to keep an eye on the scoring rate, and to make sure they're in with a chance of picking up some worthwhile prize money. All this tends to make English first-class cricket a bit of a business sometimes, and if you're out of form and unsure of your place in the side it can be a hard, unyielding slog.

But we umpires do have our problems as well. There's gamesmanship for a start. I believe cricket should be played in a sporting spirit within the rules at all times — and there's no doubt in my mind that gamesmanship is on the increase. Ninety per cent of the players in first-class cricket don't walk any more; they stand there and wait to be given out. It's not so bad at county level where there's still a spirit of good fellowship, but in Tests there are no favours. You're playing for your country, you desperately want to do well, and if you're out — well, let's see what the umpire thinks. I'd prefer a batsman to walk if he knew he was out but I'd also like consistency. The problems arise when a batsman who usually walks stays at the crease when he knows he's out. This may be because he's having a bad run (and moral considerations tend to go out of the window when a place in the side is at stake), but that doesn't make the umpire's job any easier. I can understand the Australian view — the umpire is there to decide, and no complaints if he gives you out, but on no account help him make up his mind. At least their players are consistent, although personally I like to see old-fashioned qualities like sportsmanship now and again.

I remember a graphic example of sportsmanship when I first played for Kent in 1961. I was batting with John Prodger against Somerset when he went to cut Ken Palmer and the ball brushed his glove *en route* to the wicket-keeper. Nobody appealed because there was no sound or deviation — but John didn't hesitate and walked off. Early in my umpiring career an outstanding example of sportsmanship was shown by Essex's Brian Ward in a match against Warwickshire. Lance Gibbs bowled and the ball turned and lifted, touching his glove on the way to leg slip, who caught the ball. Nobody appealed, but just as Lance was about to bowl again we saw Brian Ward walking back to the pavilion. Only *he* knew he'd 'gloved' the ball, and when the Warwickshire captain, Alan Smith, called out, 'Well walked, Brian', everybody realized what a fine gesture it was.

The overseas players in county cricket don't walk. That's the way they've been brought up and at least we umpires know where we stand. I'm a fan of the great overseas players and I feel it's a privilege to see them play at close quarters, but there's no doubt that they've introduced a competitive element into English cricket that sometimes spills over into gamesmanship and intimidation. I think the structure of overseas cricket has something to do with their occasionally explosive temperaments.

In South Africa and Australia sporting feelings are bottled up until the weekend when all hell is let loose, no quarter is asked or given on the field of play, and everyone has a drink together afterwards. The average county pro in England, on the other hand, couldn't sustain such sheer aggression day in, day out all season, so he has to pace himself temperamentally. In addition, the English county player is a fairly placid person. He's learned his trade at the hands of experienced, grizzled old pros and he's told at an early stage that the umpire is in charge during play. Overseas it's said that the umpiring standards aren't as high and so players get more frustrated and undisciplined.

But there is more aggro and frustration on the field in English first-class cricket these days — partly due to the financial rewards, partly due to the philosophy of our times, the influence of the overseas players and also the nature of our wickets. These days everybody can bat a bit, and on slow, flat wickets a decent tail-ender can prop one end up for a long time. That's when the fast bowlers get mad — the wicket's not helping them, they're tired, they want a rest and this bloke keeps blocking everything. Then the bouncers start — though not against the good batsman, because he can punish them.

Chatting away at batsmen is a fairly new department in the gamesmanship catalogue. This happens at Test level, rather than in the county game where people bump into each other a lot during a season and therefore don't try it on too much. In Tests, it's done fairly subtly so that neither umpire can hear the 'verbals' coming from the wicket-keeper or the close fielders. If ever I hear it, I step in straight away and tell them to cut out the nonsense, but the remarks are usually low enough to be out of our earshot. Two men who've picked up quite a reputation for this kind of trick are Tony Greig and Ian Chappell. They've both been accused of lowering the standards of behaviour on the field but I can only speak as I find, and neither of them was any trouble to me. Greigy played it hard, as a typical South African will, but he never gave me any backchat or put pressure on a batsman as far as I could tell. Chappell really got his team

in order whenever I umpired — I've seen him tell Dennis Lillee to get back to his bowling mark when Lillee's followed through and tried to 'eyeball' a batsman who was giving him some trouble. I know Chappell has had his moments in Australia, but perhaps his discipline over his teams while touring this country was his way of telling the English umpires that we weren't all that bad at our jobs.

I don't like all this chattering: it's difficult to work out who's doing it. I also don't like the habit of shouting 'Catch it!' if the ball has hit the batsman's pads and it balloons harmlessly into a close fielder's hands. Perhaps it's just a nervous reaction to the ball being in the air, even though the bat was nowhere near the ball — but if it ever gets out of hand, I tell the fielders to cut it out. I remember standing in one county match with that fine Australian umpire Tom Brooks when he spent a season in England. He was disturbed by all the 'Catch its' that were flying around and I advised him to crack down at his end. He did so and that was the end of it — but the players shouldn't really even try to get away with it.

All an umpire has to do is assert his authority whenever necessary. In first-class cricket some players will try to 'psych' you out, but they leave the umpire alone as soon as they realize they won't get anywhere with such tactics. They can appeal as much as they like, but if I think the appeals are getting ridiculous, the tone of my voice when dismissing the appeal will make my opinions quite clear. There's no need to be ostentatious about this — just be firm at the right moment and the players won't take too many liberties. As in any walk of life, where there's discipline and a sensible show of authority, the situation can be calm and orderly.

When you *do* grant an appeal, try to stop your finger coming up like a bolt from the blue. I'm not sure what constitutes a sensible interval, because I've watched replays on TV when I've been positive I bulleted someone out, only to be surprised by the amount of time I took. But if you wait *too* long, the players will think you're indecisive. Broadly speaking, I would say that

28

your first reaction is the right one: either he's in or he's out, as simple as that, and don't spend all day deliberating the pros and cons.

An umpire will create pressures for himself if he gives 'make up' decisions — in other words he's thought about a not out he's given and realized it was the wrong decision, so he decides to redress the balance as soon as possible. That's wrong. Every ball must be taken on its merits and you must give what you see. John Edrich was a great man for concentrating on the next ball and forgetting that the previous one had nearly bowled him all ends up. A player and an umpire are only expected to deal with one ball at a time — but as soon as word spreads that a particular umpire gives 'make up' decisions he'll have to deal with more appeals than Dr Barnardo ever experienced!

Never be afraid to consult your fellow umpire. Mistakes happen when an umpire tries to run the game on his own and forgets he can get advice from his colleague about bad light, the bounce of the wicket or a bowler's illegal delivery. Nobody knows everything, but between the two of you there's a good chance you can get most things right. And there's no such thing as a senior umpire — the other bloke may have been at it longer but you still have to give decisions at your end even if it's your first match.

Don't consult with your fellow umpire because you don't want to give a decision. I only call him in if I didn't see the catch cleanly taken and the other fellow may have had a clear view. This happened to me in my first Test at Leeds in 1971. Pakistan's Intikhab bowled to Alan Knott who came down the wicket, misjudged the flight and dabbed the ball to Zaheer at first slip. Arthur Fagg had been impeded by the bowler's follow-through so he called me in from square leg. I saw it clearly, so Knotty was on his way. In the same year, Bill Alley helped me out in the Hampshire v. Pakistanis match. Saeed Ahmed hit one to square leg, who dived and caught it very near the ground. I couldn't see and Saeed stood his ground — but fortunately Bill saw it all the way from his position at square leg and ruled that it was a straightforward catch. But don't forget — the other umpire is only there to confirm what you haven't been able to see, not to make up his colleague's hesitant mind for him.

Sometimes there'll be pressure on you to justify a decision. Resist that pressure and tell the player concerned where to get off in no uncertain terms. Tell him you don't discuss your decisions on the field of play but that you have been known to talk about things over a pint afterwards. I faced this problem in one of my early Tests — at Trent Bridge in 1973 against New Zealand. Bev Congdon, the tourists' skipper, was bowling to Alan Knott and he appealed for lbw. In fact Knotty got an inside edge to the delivery but I didn't see why I should tell the bowler that. At the end of the over, Congdon said, 'Did he get a nick on that?' and I replied, 'I don't discuss my decisions, captain, I gave him not out and that's the end of it.' Later in the match, the Kiwis' wicket-keeper Ken Wadsworth was given out by me — caught Knott, bowled Greig. He obviously wasn't too happy with the decision because he swished his bat angrily as he walked out. At the interval I went into the New Zealand dressing-room and said to Congdon, 'Captain, I don't want any of your players showing dissent — that's not the way we play over here.' After that Congdon and I never really got on, but I stand by my attitude — and I think every umpire should do the same.

If someone comes up after the day's play is over and quietly asks for my view on a decision, that's different, and I've often enjoyed those quiet little chats with sincere players who aren't out to undermine the umpire's authority but nevertheless want to know the way our minds work. Such players — the ones who get on with the game without fuss and never pressurize the umpire — are happily in the majority in English first-class cricket. They all get het-up at times, but normally their anger is directed at themselves for their own inadequacies. Umpires get to know the personalities of the 'star' names; they see how they react under stress and it's comparatively easy to sort out the nice blokes from the bad ones. The relationship between

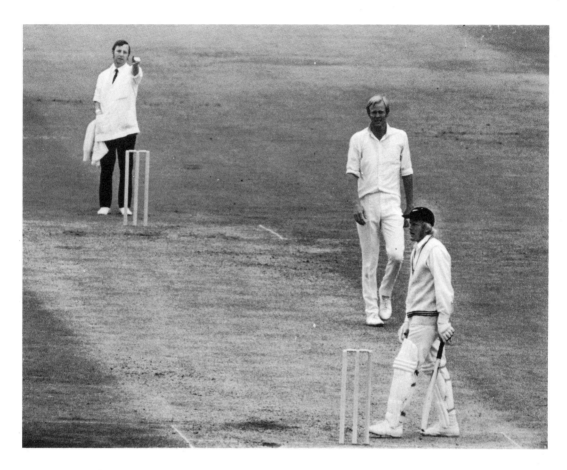

players and umpires in England is still good because most
players realize that we have a difficult job to do, that most of us
used to play the game at first-class level, and that without a
basis of authority the game itself suffers. But even at social
functions the umpire shouldn't approach a player to discuss the
day's play; he should wait until he's asked his opinion and only
then talk in detail about something specific. Sometimes a player
who's down in the dumps doesn't want to get involved in chit-
chat with the umpire who's given him out, so we should respect
his wishes and leave him alone.

I suppose TV is considered one of the main pressures on an umpire at Test or county level, but I personally don't find that. I believe the action replay proves the umpire right more often than not and I have no real complaints about the way I've been treated. I think television does a good job on dismissals because I'm always interested to see how someone got out — whether he's played down the wrong line, or if the ball's deviated, or how the fielder was positioned for the catch he subsequently dropped. Mind you, television has proved I've made mistakes in Tests — one was at Leeds in the 1972 England v. Australia match. Peter Parfitt was batting, Dennis Lillee bowling, and I heard a noise and gave him out, caught behind by Marsh. There was no doubt at all in my mind and Parfitt, like a typical old pro, took it well and marched off without even a glance. But as soon as I walked in through the door at home my wife told me, 'He was nowhere near it, the television proved that.' Fair enough — but I had to judge honestly on the evidence available at the time.

Another mistake happened at Trent Bridge in the 1973 Test against New Zealand, when Ken Wadsworth played a ball from Geoff Arnold to backward short leg where Norman Gifford took the catch. I said 'Not out', but I learned afterwards I was wrong. Then there was the 1971 Test at Lord's against India when I gave Viswanath out, caught at short leg off Norman Gifford, when the ball hit his pad. Nor must I forget Bob Willis in 1978 at the Oval against New Zealand. All the Kiwis thought the wicket-keeper had caught him off Richard Hadlee. I disagreed, even though all the fielders started to walk off at what they thought was the end of the innings. I watched the TV action replay that night and the loud nick, the ball's deviation and the reaction of the close fielders convinced me I was wrong.

Then there was my biggest error — when I gave Alan Knott out lbw in the Trent Bridge Test of 1980 against the West Indies. Alan misjudged the bounce, allowed it to hit his elbow and for a split second all my training went out the window. The line was completely wrong and it was my worst-ever decision. Luckily Alan took it magnificently, but I could have died on the spot.

I make that a total of five mistakes in my Tests — and it took TV to convince me I was in the wrong. No complaints from me about any suggestions of 'trial by television', because I maintain any umpire with confidence in himself and honesty of purpose has nothing to fear from the cameras — indeed he can learn from them. I'm not so sure about newspaper coverage, though — too much that is trivial is included, and I get frustrated by the newspapers because I know there is so much that's worthwhile about modern cricket that just gets ignored. I don't blame the cricket reporters — it's more the fault of their sports editors, who want sensationalism, or a fresh angle to a story when one doesn't necessarily exist.

The main thing that worries me about TV coverage is the fact that some of the less desirable habits of a minority of players are likely to be copied on the school or village field. Cricket is no different from any other sport in that impressionable youngsters will try to emulate their heroes in everything, including behaviour. I know there are pressures on the modern cricketer, but I don't like to switch on my television and see bowlers give V signs to the crowd, or batsmen and bowlers exchanging angry words in close-up. I know such things regrettably happen, and it's judged bad television if you see nothing but good-tempered cricketers exchanging friendly words between overs . . . but I sometimes worry about the standards of behaviour we are setting for tomorrow's cricketers. Umpires have no powers to send a player off the field for bad behaviour, and please God it never comes to that. I would like to see something like the ice hockey 'sin bin', so that a bowler who persistently runs on to the wicket or a chattering close fielder could be taken out of the next two-hour session. That way the offender's team suffers and mature, sporting behaviour gets its reward, especially when the punished player is the team's star fast bowler. The same would apply to a batsman who deliberately cuts up the wicket to help his side's spinners late in the game.

Generally, however, the behaviour of English cricketers at all levels is pretty good. There's no point in being complacent because anyone with a grain of common sense should know that at least a couple of men out of 22 will be different from the rest. They may think the umpire's weak or short-sighted or lacking in knowledge or simply incompetent. It's up to the umpire to give that small minority no cause for complaint, and if there's trouble it can be just as much the fault of the umpire who lacks the guts to take on the offender or to assert his authority and let the captain know what's going on. If that's pressure on an umpire, fair enough, but if he can't take it, he shouldn't be out there in the middle.

# 3 Tricky Decisions and Oddities

The laws of the game are quite simple once you've waded through them and grasped their significance — but there are occasions when a little teaser crops up or when you have to be particularly vigilant. I'm often asked what are the trickiest decisions to make. The weather conditions, if I've managed to get a clear sight of the ball and if I've had co-operation from my fellow umpire or the fielders determine whether it's a tricky decision. The ideal weather for umpiring is a still, calm day with a bright light, but no glare. There'll be no wind to play tricks on your hearing, you won't have to peer through the gloom to see where the ball's landed, and you're not dazzled by the sun.

Apart from the vexed question of lbw, I suppose catches exercise an umpire most. They come in various categories but you need the same assets to adjudicate properly — a keen eye, a sound pair of ears, a calm mind and enough common sense to know when there's a bit of gamesmanship at work from either the batsman or the fielding side.

One of the most difficult decisions is the bat/pad catch. These are becoming more and more common now that the fielders are able to wear helmets which allow them to creep nearer and nearer to the bat. One man is stationed close on the leg side for the ball that's turned into the batsman, who can't keep it down. There's usually another man on the off side in case the ball pops up in that area — in both cases the umpire has to be really alert to watch the ball, to see and, if possible, hear

a deflection. Don't focus your eyes on the pad, even though that should be near the bat; watch the ball on to the bat. Be ready to follow the ball from the bat and don't anticipate. I remember one Test I stood in when I expected a thick inside edge from Geoff Miller to end up at short leg — instead it popped out on the off side to silly mid-off where Pakistan's Javed Miandad caught it low to his right. There were fieldsmen all around the bat — which is a visual distraction on its own — and I needed to discipline myself to watch where the ball *was* heading, rather than where I *expected* it to go.

Watch out for the 'catch it' treatment. I can give some eager fielders the benefit of the doubt sometimes and put such cries down to keenness, but not all the time. Just because they're telling you there's been a snick and the ball's in the air doesn't mean you should react accordingly. Remember that you're in the best position to judge, your ears must work with your eyes, and other people's opinions are irrelevant. The mental strain is greater when the spinners are operating because you don't have a chance to switch off for a short time and get the circulation going in the legs, as with the fast bowlers. But it's a rewarding

36

thing to see the spinners in action and I enjoy the contest and try to keep a clear head all the time.

Catches in the slips can be tricky, especially on grounds where the square is raised because it's been built up with topsoil over the years, so that the square dips away a few yards past the batsman's stumps. In such circumstances you have to watch a snick closely, especially if it's keeping low on the way to the slips or the wicket-keeper. It may be that you can't see the catch all the way, so you have to call in the square-leg umpire to confirm whether or not the ball carried. Leeds and the Oval are a problem in this respect — I remember Bob Taylor catching New Zealand's Brendon Bracewell at the Oval in 1978. Bob Willis bowled a pretty sharp delivery, Bracewell nicked it fast and low, and Taylor had to dive forward to catch it very near the ground. It was a fine catch, and I was pleased with my decision because I followed it all the way (despite the dip in the square) and I resisted the temptation to relax subconsciously and think, 'Oh, he'll never get to that one.'

I find that the better the keeper the more difficult the decision, because you have to stop yourself from relaxing your concentration. If a batsman gets a thin edge on to his pads and the ball travels fast and wide, you tend to think, 'He won't get that,' only to see a Knott or a Taylor travel a couple of yards in record time and snaffle the catch while you're in the process of relaxing.

Leg-side catches to the keeper can be tricky for visual reasons. The batsman gets tucked up, the angle is shortened, and you have to concentrate to see whether the ball touched his bat, a glove, the upper part of his body or simply went through without touching anything. In many cases the keeper won't know, but that won't stop him appealing for the catch! Catches off the glove are particularly tricky because there won't be much deviation and you have to rely on the sound as much as anything. Good hearing is also vital in the case of an inside edge to the keeper — for a split second you lose sight of the ball as it passes between the bat's edge and the stumps.

*A fine, low catch by Bob Taylor that needed all my concentration because there was a slight dip in the ground past the stumps and the ball was dropping all the way. But I sighted it quickly and followed it. The unlucky batsman is New Zealand's Brendon Bracewell and the happy bowler is Bob Willis*

One tip for the batsman who feels aggrieved at several alleged catches by the keeper — take a look at your bat. Many batsmen are loath to change a favourite old bat, even though the handle is creaking badly. A creak in the handle or the splice sounds awfully like a nick from 22 yards away, and you don't really expect the umpire to have the hearing of a cat, do you? We're only human. . . .

Another vexed problem with these type of catches is in defining whether the ball grazed the wrist. Law 35 states that anything *below* the wrist is deemed an extension of the bat and is therefore out, while anything *on or above* the wrist is not out. The difficulty lies in spotting the precise area of the ball's impact, especially when the fast bowlers are operating. Concentrate, look, listen and concentrate again.

Wicket-keepers also cause us problems with stumpings. The eyes have to take in the whole scene — the bowler's delivery, the speed of the ball, the position of the batsman's feet, the keeper's hands, when he breaks the wicket — and was the ball still in his hands when he broke the wicket? Imagine what it's like with a bowler like Derek Underwood; batsmen keep telling me how difficult it is to get after a man of his pace, but it's also pretty difficult to umpire with him around!

*Stumpings can be tricky for the square-leg umpire because he has to take a lot in — the bowler's delivery, the position of the batsman's feet and the keeper's hands when he breaks the wicket. Here India's Reddy gets it right and Ian Botham is out*

Slip catches can be tricky when the keeper obscures your view and you're not really sure whether the ball carried. As a general principle, just follow the ball and see where it ends up, but when in doubt call in the square-leg umpire. I recall giving out Majid Khan when he was batting for Cambridge University against Leicestershire. Graham McKenzie bowled, Majid snicked it to Barry Dudleston at second slip, but unfortunately McKenzie obscured my vision in his follow-through. I called in Alan Whitehead and he saw it all the way from his square-leg vantage-point and I gave Majid out.

Watch out for catches to leg slip. Because you can't really move your position at the bowler's end due to the need to be ready to adjudicate in an lbw appeal, you have to hope you can follow the ball and that it will be high enough in the air to avoid being obscured by the batsman or short leg. For a split second you probably won't be able to see the ball, but at least leg-slip catches are, like ones to slip, fairly slow-moving, and hopefully you'll have time to resight the flight of the ball. If not, enter the square-leg umpire yet again. . . .

Then there are caught and bowled decisions. These can be difficult when the bowler has his back to you and dives at an angle for a low catch. Watch out for the give-away sound of the ball thudding on the ground and the disappointed reaction of the bowler and close fielders if the ball's been grassed. Above all, if you can't be certain about the catch, the batsman stays in.

In these days of spectacular reactions to catches, where the ball is thrown sky-high in exultation almost as soon as it's grasped, I'm often asked how long a catch must be in the hands before it's valid. The common sense answer to that one is that it's a catch when the fielder is deemed to have the ball under control. And if he's thrown the ball up almost immediately, you can assume he must have had the ball under his control.

So much for catches. Another thing that bothers club and school umpires is the no-ball rule — many don't really understand it, and to avoid trouble they tend to ignore the rule. I believe that's wrong, because a bowler is getting an unfair

OPPOSITE *Two examples of the difficulties umpires face when the bowler partially obscures his vision for a slip catch. In the photograph above, Barrie Meyer has to take a step round New Zealand's Richard Hadlee to judge if the snick from Warwickshire's Neal Abberley carried to Mark Burgess. It did. In the photograph below, Dennis Lillee partially blocks Derek Underwood's edge to Ian Chappell. If the umpire has any doubts at all, he should call in his colleague at square leg*

40

advantage by delivering the ball too near to the batsman. Mind you, I'm not too keen on the present no-ball rule which states that some part of the bowler's front foot must be behind the popping crease, compared with the old rule which said that some part of the back foot had to be behind the crease containing the stumps. That gave the umpire more time to see the ball after checking the position of the bowler's feet — now we have to adjust very quickly and sometimes the keeper's throwing the ball back before you've really sighted a very quick delivery. (The diagram below illustrates the no-ball rule.)

In my opinion, no professional cricketer should bowl a no-ball. He should know where his feet are going and where the crease is positioned, no matter how quickly he's bowling. The trouble is that they don't get much chance to sort out their run-ups in the nets because often the creases aren't marked properly. Rhythm is very important to fast bowlers and you can always tell when they're really putting something into the job in hand by the way they approach the crease and hammer the front foot down. If the rhythm is wrong, the no-balls start coming. The West Indian Keith Boyce was the worst in my experience. He used to bowl about 250 of them every season when he first came over to Essex. Poor old 'Lofty' Herman of Hampshire used to struggle as well — he'd be all over the place on occasions because he didn't know where his feet were landing. Now that he's on the first-class umpires' list, it'll be interesting to hear his views on the no-ball rule! Geoff Arnold

LEFT *Fair ball — part of the bowler's front foot is behind the popping/crease line*

RIGHT *No-ball — the bowler's front foot is completely in front of the popping/crease line*

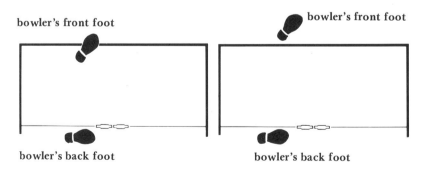

bowler's front foot

bowler's front foot

bowler's back foot

bowler's back foot

42

used to give me headaches when he was bowling because he was usually within half an inch of the line. A very precise bowler, Geoff always knew where his feet were landing. Often a fast bowler will say to me, 'Give us a shout if I start creeping up,' and I'm always happy to do so, but never be tempted to sympathize with a bowler and let him off the hook. He is infringing the laws of the game and gaining an unfair advantage.

An even more tricky no-ball decision concerns throwing. Now I'll be honest, I think it's very difficult to spot a throw with the naked eye. If I've ever had any doubts about the bowler's bent arm straightening in the delivery, I've reported it to Lord's and let them film that man. I think many slow bowlers may throw the ball a little because they're using a slightly bent arm to get leverage. I can't see how you can spin the ball with a straight arm. But I'm happy to leave such problems to the cameras.

43

*One of those oddities that occasionally delight everyone but the dismissed batsman. The match was in 1971, between Cambridge University and the University Athletics Union. The UAU keeper, Derryck Murray, has completed the formality of breaking the wicket — but who's been run out, the diving Phil Edmonds or Peter Johnson? The man out was Johnson. He was the non-striker and the umpire felt that Edmonds had not advanced sufficiently down the wicket to have 'crossed'. Would you have ruled the same?*

The umpire at club or schoolboy level is more likely to have problems with wides than with throws. An important point here is to remember that interpretation is vital; it all depends on the size of the batsman. A ball that goes *outside* the return crease may not be a wide to a man with the long reach of a Clive Lloyd, whereas a ball a foot *inside* the return crease could be a wide to a small man like Harry Pilling. The ability to reach the ball is the crucial factor — if the ball is *beyond* the batsman's reach, it's a wide, simple as that. And take no notice of the look of consternation on the bowler's face. Most of them take it as a personal insult, a blow to their skills, if they bowl a wide. That's

44

no concern of yours — you're there to be fair to everyone, and
that includes a batsman who can't get to a ball because it's
outside his reach.

Despite the precise nature of the laws of cricket, there are
occasions when some humorous oddities appear. I remember
standing in a county match at Worcester when the home
skipper, Norman Gifford, was embarrassed. The match against
Northamptonshire was reduced to two days because of rain, and
Norman forgot that in such cases the follow-on is reduced from
150 to 100 runs. Norman declared 140 runs behind, thinking he
could then have a crack at the Northants batting, only to be

told by his opposing captain, Jim Watts, 'Off you go and bat again, Norman.' Fortunately it didn't have a vital bearing on the game, but Norman's wry comment that he'd better get back to the Second XI to learn the laws of the game went down well. I couldn't volunteer the information during Worcester's first innings unless Norman had asked me, because an umpire is there to carry out the laws. But I had a slight chuckle to myself when Norman declared, because I knew what was coming up next!

Different grounds have different characteristics and it's important to know about them before play starts. At Lord's the boundary on one side is a fence, on the other a rope. At Canterbury, if the ball hits the famous tree it's a four, even though it's well within the field of play. And the clock can go wrong; the one at Hove is deceptive — it always gains on the downswing and loses on the upswing, although it eventually comes right at the top of the hour! The umpires should always synchronize their watches at the start of the day so that if the pavilion clock goes wrong they can go by their own watches. Basically the umpires must inform both captains about the position of the boundaries, the hours of play, which clock is the one that regulates the playing hours, and any other local conditions of relevance.

One important thing for all umpires to remember: Law 46 is your safety valve in the event of any dissent or trouble. It's a broad regulation but basically it means that the umpires are the sole judges of what constitutes unfair or ungentlemanly conduct. Obviously that's something rarely used in first-class cricket, but if someone persists in behaving badly on the village green or in a schools match, Law 46 is there to enable the umpire to say, 'Pack it in — that's not fair.' I think it's a good rule to brandish at those who just don't know *how* to play the game and think they can be judge and jury as well as player. It can be used in cases like persistent and unnecessary appealing, chattering at the batsman to try to put him off, or back-chat from the batsman to the bowler who's lost his confidence and hardly knows where his next delivery is going to land.

OPPOSITE *An incident that needed all my vigilance to give the right decision. India's Vengsarkar edged Bob Willis to wicket-keeper David Barstow, who nudged it to Ian Botham at second slip via Mike Brearley's boot at first slip*

46

A satisfying decision by me in the England v. Australia Test at Leeds in 1972. Rod Marsh 'gloved' a ball from Derek Underwood that turned and bounced and Alan Knott caught it down the leg side. Only a faint noise and plenty of close fielders to distract me, but I picked up the deflection and the sound early

Every umpire worth his salt occasionally looks back and allows himself a quiet pat on the back for some good decisions or reactions to a few oddities. I'm no exception and, having confessed my five big mistakes in Tests, I now intend to redress the balance.

I was pleased with a decision I gave in the Lord's Test of 1976 between England and the West Indies. Barry Wood 'gloved' Michael Holding to the wicket-keeper, Deryck Murray. Barry took a slight step to go but nobody appealed. I had already given him out in my own mind but couldn't reveal what I knew. Then Clive Lloyd appealed from gully and I gave him out. It was one of those rare occasions when I and the non-striker (Chris Old) knew what had happened but the fielders didn't, and I was pleased I'd spotted the slight deflection.

Then there was that much-photographed incident in the Test

against the Indians at the Oval in 1979. Vengsarkar edged Bob Willis to David Bairstow behind the stumps, who knocked it on to Mike Brearley at first slip; the ball hit his instep and rebounded to Ian Botham's safe hands at second slip. It was a tricky one to follow because the ball went to three different places, but luckily it was a fairly thick edge from the batsman. At close of play, several people said 'How did you follow that one?' and it was one of the rare occasions when an umpire's ability can be seen by the spectators.

Another wicket-keeper's catch gratified me — at Leeds in 1972. Australia's Rod Marsh got a glove to a ball that turned and bounced and Alan Knott took it on the leg side. There was hardly any noise, but fielders were all round the bat, contributing to potential distraction, yet I saw it all the way and gave Marsh out.

An umpire's job is particularly gratifying when he and the players know he's made the right decision in a tricky situation. But really the principles are the same whatever the problem — concentrate, look, listen, be decisive when your mind is made up, trust your reactions, and if the intimidation or histrionics get out of hand, there's always Law 46!

# 4 The lbw Law

Now here's a thorny topic that occupies the minds of cricketers from the village green to the Test arena; it's the worst way of getting out because it always seems so unsatisfactory. Better the slog halfway down the wicket and a catch in the deep than a defensive poke with your pads in front. No batsman knows what was likely to happen to the ball if his pads hadn't been in the way — it's only an umpire's opinion that the ball would have hit the wicket.

The club player may look forward to his game all week, only to be shot out unluckily by a dozy umpire who has merely a nodding acquaintance with the lbw laws. I believe the tail-enders at all levels of cricket suffer most. It's human nature, I suppose, but the umpires who have got used to saying 'Not out' when the top batsmen are at the crease end up lapsing subconsciously into granting appeals near the end of the innings. It drips away like water from a leaky tap, and 'make up' decisions are always possible when a few lbw appeals are made. Even in first-class cricket I think the tail-enders get seen off too often by lbw appeals that their more talented batting colleagues would avoid. I feel that too many lbw appeals are granted at all levels of the game; there's been an increase in appeals, but that doesn't mean they are correspondingly justified. I turn down more lbw appeals than I grant and I don't see any reason to change.

The top players in first-class cricket agonize over lbws

because it's all a matter of opinion, with no hard facts to back up the umpire's decision. I can understand their frustration when they're given out lbw without playing a shot, but the batsman's error of judgment isn't the umpire's fault. Batsmen keep looking at their pads in relation to the line of the stumps after they've been given out, and a few gesticulate with the bat to suggest that they touched the ball before it hit the pad. That kind of reaction is getting more prevalent in first-class cricket and I disapprove of it. The old pros were more philosophical, even just a few years ago when I was a county player — they realized that things evened themselves out over the season and tried to give the umpire as little trouble as possible. It's up to today's captains to crack down on a batsman's dissent whenever it occurs, because the umpire will always have the last word as long as there are laws on playing the game. I think a lot of today's first-class players don't really know where their stumps are when the ball is on its way; too many are on the move, so that when they're caught plumb in front and an lbw appeal is granted, they think they know best about the ball's progress. They don't. Time after time a county batsman will come to me at close of play and say, 'I had to play that one when I was

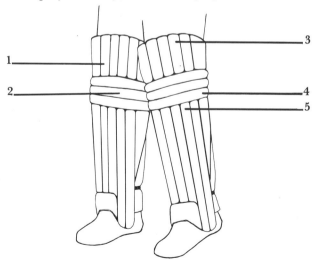

*This diagram shows the points of impact on a batsman's pads which determine whether or not an lbw appeal will be successful.*
*1. Not out — the point of impact is not in a straight line between wicket and wicket*
*2. Out — the ball would have hit the wicket, in line with the other wicket, but make sure the ball was not swinging or turning so sharply as to miss the stumps completely*
*3. Out — but the umpire may feel the ball was rising too sharply and passing over the stumps*
*4. Out — the ball pitched between wicket and wicket, although the umpire may feel the ball was turning or swinging too much and would therefore miss the off stump*
*5. Not out — the ball pitched outside the line of the leg stump*

51

caught at slip, didn't I?' and they genuinely don't realize that the ball was a fair way outside the off stump and could have been ignored. The same applies to lbws, and I've got no time for the lament: 'But that was going down the leg side.'

The great players like Tom Graveney, Geoff Boycott, Colin Cowdrey, Ken Barrington and Peter May knew where their stumps were. They played straight through the V (the area between mid-off and mid-on) and they would soon know when they were caught with their pads in front. Perhaps there aren't many great English batsmen around these days. . . .

I suppose it's easy to say this, because I'm umpiring all season, but I honestly find an lbw is the easiest decision an umpire has to make. Now I can almost hear you club cricket umpires saying, 'But what about the bounce, the different angles from over or round the wicket, the position of the front foot when the ball hits it?' As far as I'm concerned, a successful lbw appeal comprises these elements:

1. The ball pitched in line with both sets of stumps or outside the off stump.

2. The ball struck the batsman's pad or person and *not* the bat.

3. The batsman's pads or person were between the stumps at either end at the moment of impact.

4. The ball would have hit the wicket.

5. The batsman made no attempt to play a ball *outside* the off stump, it hit his pad or person, and, in the umpire's opinion, the ball would have gone on to hit the wicket.

The 'person' is defined as the batsman's body or arm which doesn't hold the bat — but not the hand which is holding the bat. So if a batsman misjudges a ball which he thinks is going to bounce, but it keeps low and hits the batsman as he ducks, then he's out lbw if the above provisos are met. It doesn't necessarily involve the pad.

There are two basic dilemmas in assessing lbw — it's all the umpire's opinion and there is a very narrow margin of error. You've got to remember the wicket is only nine inches wide and

28 inches high; if the batsman pushes forward a yard, you add that distance to the four feet between the two creases, giving you a distance of seven feet before the ball would have reached the stumps. The ball only has to deviate a quarter of an inch over that distance to miss the wicket.

An umpire can get things wrong if he doesn't hear the bat nick the ball on to the pad and he still gives the batsman out. A lot depends on the weather; if it's blustery it affects his hearing, especially if he's dealing with just a thin inside edge on to the pad.

I think the umpire has to watch every ball on its merits and watch where the bowler's feet land so that he can judge the angle of the ball once it's delivered. He should watch the ball in flight, where it pitches in relation to both sets of stumps, then assess the ball's movement off the pitch. I've always found that an lbw doesn't *feel* right when it's a not out; I suppose it's second nature to me now after judging them all these years — I appreciate that's no consolation to the club umpire who stands just a couple of times per week. But the principles at issue are clear and straightforward.

One of the vital things to consider is the angle from where the bowler delivered the ball. If he's using the full width of the crease and the right-hand bowler pushes it *into* the batsman, from *over* the wicket, there's very little hope of an lbw decision because the ball will probably be going down the leg side. A right-arm off-spinner bowling *round* the wicket has a better chance of an lbw to the right-hand batsman when the ball's turning than if he was bowling *over* the wicket. This is because the ball will probably turn too much from over the wicket and the spin will take it past the leg stump. Ray Illingworth was a genius at controlling the spin on a turning wicket — he realized that if the ball turned too much it would miss the stumps, so he would bowl wide of the crease from round the wicket and try to straighten it into the right-hander. The more the ball's turning, the wider the good spinner will bowl to make the ball come back into the stumps rather than pass harmlessly wide.

That great West Indian off-spinner Lance Gibbs took a few seasons to grasp this when he first played for Warwickshire in the county championship. He would bowl wide of the crease from over the wicket and never got any lbws, just a few catches in the leg-trap. The batsmen were getting their pads in front, secure in the knowledge that the off-break would turn sufficiently to be certain of missing the leg stump. But as soon as he mastered the technique of bowling *round* the wicket and straightening the off-break into the right-hander, he picked up a hundred wickets in a season! Australia's Ashley Mallett worked things out more quickly — he wasn't as big a spinner as Gibbs, so he could bowl over the wicket, pitch it just outside the off stump and, knowing that he was not bowling a big off-break, he could have a good shout for lbw. Mallett mastered English conditions and worked out the umpires' attitudes better than most overseas spinners.

One thing the umpire has to watch out for when a class off-spinner is bowling is the floater. This is the ball which *doesn't* turn to leg against the right-hander, but just floats gently towards the slips or even goes straight on. A different grip is used for the floater and the umpire must be alert to its occasional appearance. It must be galling for the off-spinner when he produces the floater from over the wicket and traps the batsman plumb in front — only for the umpire who doesn't really understand what's going on to say, 'Not out'. I repeat my point about umpires needing playing experience.

The easier decisions come when you have a left-arm bowler coming *over* the wicket to a right-hand bat, or conversely a right-arm bowler from over the wicket against a left-hand batsman. If both bowlers are swinging the ball into the batsmen, an lbw decision is very much on the cards if all the obvious criteria are met. This is because the ball is holding up, it's started life going across the batsman but then held up and gone *straight* to the wicket. But if a left-armer's bowling away swingers to the right-hand batsman (or the other way round, with the right-armer slanting it *away* from the left-hander) then there's little hope of a dismissal because the ball will be going away from the edge of the bat and heading in the direction of the slips — and nowhere near the stumps.

I like the regulation which states that a batsman's out lbw if he doesn't play a shot to a ball that pitches outside the off stump and it would have hit the wicket. This helps to crack down on boring pad play. In the old days a few batsmen used to plant the pad outside the off stump, secure in the knowledge that they wouldn't be given out. That was changed to encourage the slow bowlers and make the batsmen realize that they should use the bat whenever possible, not the pad — and who can complain about that line of thinking?

One thing I implore umpires at club, village green and school level to do: be careful when the batsman's hit on the front foot and he's a long way down the wicket. I hear so many accounts of players being given out lbw when their pads are in front of the wicket, and the umpire says defensively, 'Well, the ball hit him in front of the wicket.' That's not good umpiring — the ball may have hit the pads in front of the wicket, but if the batsman is tall and he's playing *well forward*, the ball has a long way to travel before it hits the stumps. It could end up miles down the leg side and that's no consolation to the angry batsman as he throws his pads in the dressing-room corner and asks his skipper to find a decent umpire. It's an even worse decision if the ball's swinging or turning a fair amount, because the 9 x 28 inch wicket can look very small when a large pad comes seven feet down the track and the ball is deviating a great deal.

How can an umpire improve his judgment of lbws? During a session I try to reassure myself about the angle of the delivery. I stop myself from prejudging, but several times I'll take a couple of paces over to the spot from where the bowler's delivering and look at the angle needed to hit the stumps. It's a case of programming myself into a decision if all the requirements are met — but only then. In the event of a full toss, I have to work out just how much the ball is swinging through the air, especially in the last part of the trajectory. Is the ball

straightening up in the air or is it boomeranging all over the place? If it's the former, there's a chance of an lbw decision.

The keen umpire who's willing to learn can try to improve his judgment in the indoor nets during the winter. Stand at the bowler's end and make a point of watching where the ball pitched and how far it deviated off the wicket. Look at the ball's movement through the air and tell yourself which ones are certain lbws and which ones are not. Then stand at the side of the net to judge the bounce, and keep telling yourself that if the ball is bouncing a lot it's fairly certain to go *over* the stumps and therefore the batsman wouldn't be lbw. Then position yourself directly behind the batsman and see where the ball ends up when he misses it. All of this helps to keep you in mental trim, to sharpen up your reflexes and awareness. Never doubt that an umpire at any standard needs to get back into the swing of things at the start of the season. It's not just a matter of putting on the white coat, indulging in a spot of banter *en route* to the middle and calling 'Play.' The more work you put into umpiring, the better you become.

Don't allow yourself to be intimidated by strident appeals for lbw from the bowler or the wicket-keeper. And if the appeals

56

come from any other fielder, that's a nonsense — how can they possibly judge the validity of an lbw appeal from gully or short leg? The keeper can see the ball up to the last couple of yards and then it's obscured by the batsman. He may have a good idea where the ball was heading but he isn't in a good position to spot the deviation, if any. The bowler is in a better position than the keeper to judge, but once he's fallen away after delivering the ball, he's too wide of the line between the stumps to get an accurate picture. The umpire is in the best position of all to judge an lbw appeal, and provided he's efficient, calm and consistent in his attitudes to the lbw regulations the players should have no complaints.

Whenever I talk at any length about lbws I can't help mentioning Gary Gilmour's match in 1975. It was the Prudential World Cup at Leeds between England and Australia and Gilmour swung the ball all over the place. I had to deal with a lot of lbw appeals that day and I gave six men out, four Englishmen and two Australians. That night I lay in bed savouring the day's play because I was pleased with my decisions. Having said that, Gilmour was easy — a left-arm swing bowler coming over the wicket and dipping the ball into the right-handers. Meat and drink to an umpire — I wish all the decisions came as easily!

I was involved in one unusual lbw decision in a Test against Australia in 1977. Richie Robinson started out intending to leave a ball from Derek Underwood, then changed his mind and tried to play it at the last instant; the ball hit his pad, then his bat. I gave him out lbw because the pad got in the way just ahead of the bat — but it took the TV action replay to convince a few sceptics that night!

It's always interesting to check a batsman's reaction if he thinks he might be given out lbw. The canny ones will try to kick the offending pad out of the way, so that the umpire can't have a good look. They'll look anywhere but down the wicket at the umpire, and affect surprise, amazement, resignation, despair or anger, depending on the stature of the umpire, the state of the game or how near the batsman was to a century.

Gilmour's match, Leeds, 1975 — and four England batsmen are dismissed by the Gary Gilmour/David Constant combination. They are Dennis Amiss (opposite above) Keith Fletcher (opposite centre) Alan Knott (opposite below) and Frank Hayes (left)

An unusual lbw dismissal, involving Australia's Richie Robinson in the Trent Bridge Test in 1977. Derek Underwood's delivery hit the pad just before the bat, a fact that was later confirmed by the TV action replay. Nice to get one right now and again . . .

Take no notice of any of that — you're there to judge the merits of the appeal, not to be influenced by any little tricks of the trade by the batsman, bowler or keeper. I often wonder how many batsmen are convinced they're out lbw. It certainly takes some persuasion at times by the umpire, but as a former batsman myself (in case you'd forgotten!) I can understand their feelings.

I've only once seen a batsman walk for an lbw and that man was Gary Sobers. I was standing in a county match at Trent Bridge when Gary was plumb in front from a right-arm inswinger. Before I could get my finger up, he was halfway down the wicket on the way to the pavilion. I thought I'd better give him out as he passed me at the bowler's end! I wonder how many other batsmen are sometimes tempted to make such a fine gesture? Mind you, Gary was a great player — he knew where his stumps were. . . .

# 5 Umpiring in Test Cricket

It was the Third Test at Leeds between England and Pakistan. It was 1971, and at the age of twenty-nine years and seven months I was standing in a Test match. It was my proudest sporting moment and will always remain so. I'd failed to make the grade as a player and standing in a Test was the next best thing to playing in one. I'll never forget the day I was told that I'd been appointed to the panel of Test umpires – 9 November 1970. My main concern was being re-elected to the panel of first-class umpires after a two-year stint in which I'd learned a lot but was still convinced I had a long way to go. Men like John Langridge had been marvellous to me, offering advice, encouragement and sensible warnings. I was gently feeling my way into my new profession – then came the letter from Lord's.

That great umpire Sid Buller had died in the summer of 1970, which left just Arthur Fagg, Charlie Elliott and 'Dusty' Rhodes on the Test panel. I think the authorities were worried about what would happen if one of those three broke a leg or fell ill, so Tom Spencer and myself were drafted in to make the number up to five. I had all winter to savour the thought of standing in a Test. The fee was £75, but money was never a consideration. As far as I was concerned, I had one foot on the ladder, and although I was flattered, surprised and honoured at my selection, I knew I had to get many more seasons under my belt before I could claim to be a Langridge or a Buller.

On the day of my first Test the press and TV coverage was very kind to me and I was touched by several nice gestures. I asked my colleague Arthur Fagg if I could take the first ball; he realized how much that meant to me and was delighted to agree. Then Ray Illingworth, the England captain, said, 'All the best, I hope things go well for you.' But reality is always just round the corner in cricket. There I was on the morning of the match, savouring the lovely atmosphere of a Leeds Test, when one of the England players popped his head round the umpires' room and said, 'Congratulations and good luck.' Before I had the chance to reply in suitably modest terms, he said, 'Mind you, there wasn't much competition, was there?'

So to the first over of the match. Asif Masood bowled and the ball bounced three times to the wicket-keeper! He did it again next ball and I thought, 'We're going to have to call this match off, there's something wrong with the wicket, the ball's not bouncing!' I didn't realize that opening bowlers are affected by nerves and stiff muscles. The third delivery brought me into action — an lbw appeal against Geoff Boycott. No problem — not out. I was in the game at last.

I wasn't really nervous after those initial deliveries, even though it was the largest crowd I'd ever been involved with. The Yorkshire crowd were as knowledgeable as ever, and the Test match atmosphere was really something. It was a great day for, of all people, the boys from Eltham Baths in London! Four men involved in that Test had been coached at Eltham Baths many years previously — Robin Hobbs, Alan Knott, Brian Luckhurst and David Constant. What were the odds against that happening? We all had a laugh about it during the match and if I still harboured envy deep down at my mates who'd become Test players, I was nevertheless proud to play some part in a Test match.

It was a very good Test. Pakistan lost by just 25 runs when they should have strolled it — Sadiq was steering the side home to the victory target and all he needed was someone to stay with him. That man seemed to be Asif Iqbal, who played splendidly until he had a rush of blood, charged down the wicket to Gifford and I gave him out, stumped Knott. Illingworth's captaincy was first-class on that last, tense morning. He got Zaheer Abbas out first ball, caught at short leg by Luckhurst, when most pundits would have thought the skipper would do the conventional thing and open the attack with the seamers. But he knew what he was doing — he preyed on the nerves of the young Pakistani batsmen, then brought in his pace bowlers, and the tail collapsed like a pack of cards.

I gave one interesting decision in this match. It happened in the Pakistan first innings when Sadiq played forward to Gifford's left-arm spin. The ball got wedged between bat and thigh, it popped forward and Knott dived and took it inches from the ground. Full marks to Knotty's anticipation — and I was pleased to realize that, even though I'd played for years in the Kent Second XI with him, he was just another pair of keeper's gloves when it came to my making a decision.

I loved everything about that first Test of mine but I wasn't prepared for the after-effects. On the final day I travelled from Leeds to Scarborough to stand in the Yorkshire v. Derbyshire county match. It was only when I was out there in the middle on the Wednesday that it hit me how shattered I was. In the first over Geoff Boycott called Barry Leadbeater for a quick single, and although my mind was telling me to get side-on of the wicket at the bowler's end, I found my legs just couldn't carry me to the right position. I was washed out in that match, both physically and mentally. Thankfully I haven't had such an experience since, and the Test umpires always have three days' rest after the end of a Test match, a ruling that I believe is absolutely right. If we umpires aren't up to the mark, how can you expect the players to do their best and abide by our rulings? I feel very sorry for the Test players, who have to get their concentration and keenness back to a peak for their county just after a Test has come to a gripping conclusion.

My next Test was equally dramatic. It came in that same 1971 season, it was at Lord's, and it involved the Indians. What

64

an atmosphere Lord's provides in a Test match! On the Saturday of that match there were 20,000 spectators, and although only 133 runs were scored by the Indians I neither noticed nor cared. Illingworth and Gifford were bowling a lot, and when the spinners are on the umpire always has to concentrate extra hard, especially on a wicket like this one where the ball turned on the first morning. It was tight, competitive cricket and I think this match and the previous one at Leeds were ideal in helping me find my feet in Test cricket. India were 38 runs short of victory with 2 wickets in hand when the rain came down — I don't think either captain was all that worried about forcing the umpires to get out again in that last rainy hour, because there was a hell of a lot at stake.

On that final, tense day an incident occurred which I'd never previously experienced. Sunil Gavaskar and Farokh Engineer were inching the Indians towards their first-ever Test victory in England by virtue of some splendid cricket — they were stealing a few singles to bring the fielders in, then hitting a few boundaries over their heads. The game was running away from England and John Snow in particular was getting frustrated. Then Engineer took a sharp single off Snow's bowling and Snow leant on Gavaskar as he was sprinting to make good his ground and sent the little man tumbling. Snowy realized at once that he had to make a gesture to the batsman, so he threw his bat towards him. Most people thought he was throwing Gavaskar's bat *at* him, not *towards* him, and Snowy was a little unlucky that the roof subsequently fell in on him. Gavaskar — gentleman that he is — never batted an eyelid and simply got on with the job while I said to Snowy, 'None of that, remember where you're playing.' At the interval, I went into the England dressing-room and told Ray Illingworth, 'Captain, I don't want any more of that.' Ray said that Gavaskar was all set to tread on Snowy's fingers, so he had to push him out of the way to get to the ball. I told him I wanted no more of it and walked out of the dressing-room as Snowy was saying, 'It was all in the heat of the moment.' The press and television had a field day and the incident was replayed all night on the box. But the Indian players weren't at all worried and although I think John Snow was rightly dropped from the next Test as a disciplinary measure and made to apologise to the opposition, the incident wasn't a bad-tempered, vicious one. It really did all happen in the heat of the moment.

Sunil Gavaskar made a deep impression on me for another reason in that Test. Before the game started he came into the umpires' room and asked Charlie Elliott and me, 'Can you please tell me how to play in England?' Charlie said, 'Let the ball come on to your bat, don't go fishing too much for it. Leave your shot till the last possible moment.' I was surprised that such an obviously fine young batsman would seek out the umpires for advice, and I warmed to his sincerity and humility. He was in the process of breaking all sorts of batting records overseas, but he realized that no batsman is a great player until he masters English conditions. I felt that that little chat reflected great credit on Sunil Gavaskar — and on the status of the English umpire. It was nearly time to stand in a Test, yet here was the opposition's star batsman trusting our integrity and experience enough to ask our advice.

It had been a memorable introduction to Test cricket for me. There I was, lying in a lovely warm bath at Lord's, the head-quarters of cricket. I'd just umpired in a Test before I was 30. It seemed a far cry from my early cricket days with Lewisham Boys' School.

My next Test in the following year was also at Lord's and it was an occasion I'll never forget. Massie's match will go down in the annals as one of the greatest displays of swing bowling ever seen in a Test — and it was his debut in Test cricket! He bowled 'banana' balls all through the match. Helped by the overcast conditions, he just ran up and bowled, and luck, his own skill and the atmosphere did the rest. He took 16 wickets in the match against a very shrewd, hard-headed, professional English batting side. It was amazing to see mature, experienced technicians like Mike Smith bowled round their legs by this man from Western Australia — and didn't the ball swing! The ball was doing so much through the air that the game would have been over on the first day if I'd granted all the appeals that came my way. England should surely have fared better against a predominantly English-style bowler, but in those days there weren't many bowlers like Massie in the English game. Snow and Price, the English opening bowlers in this Test, were typical of their breed — they'd pound in and hit the deck and try to move the ball off the seam. So their influence in such humid, swing bowler's conditions was inevitably muted.

I have so many memories from that match — Basil D'Oliveira coming to me at close of play and saying, 'When you gave me out lbw today, I thought that was wrong. But I've now seen it on the TV and you were right — that ball was swinging all over the place.' There was Greg Chappell's magnificent 131 out of 308 that effectively won the game for Australia once Massie had shown that the gods were on his side. Chappell's was a beautifully controlled, elegant, commanding innings with invaluable support from Ross Edwards, whose 28 in a couple of hours on a green wicket was worth far more than it looked in the scorebook.

In this Test I experienced my most embarrassing moment as an umpire. Bruce Francis wasn't having a very good year with the Australians. He was a hard-hitting opening batsman who kept being bowled 'through the gate' by the shrewd English bowlers, or caught behind, playing across the line. He wasn't exactly the greatest fielder to leave the shores of Australia, either. In the Lord's Test, Massie bowled to Knott who went down the wicket in typically audacious style, only to get an inside edge and chip it in the direction of mid-wicket. It was the easiest of chances — except that mid-wicket was Bruce Francis. His confidence by this time was rock-bottom, both with the bat and in the field, and he dropped the ball. I didn't know where to look, and if I tell you that the Aussies — not the most delicate of souls — were equally affected, you will realize how embarrassing it all was.

*Leeds, 1972 – with the ball turning on the first day, the England v. Australia Test was a difficult one to umpire, with close fielders hemming in the batsmen and many bat/pad appeals. Here's one I accepted – John Inverarity, caught Illingworth, bowled Underwood*

So ended Massie's match, with an 8-wicket win for the Aussies. It was a fabulous performance by Bob Massie and I still can't work out why he faded into oblivion. Perhaps he just swung the ball too much, but make no mistake about it, he was a good bowler and it would be wrong to write off the Lord's Test as simply a fluke.

I recall another great moment from that match – a crowd of 31,000 chanting 'Lillee, Lillee', 'Massie, Massie', as they both walked back to their bowling mark. As I stood there waiting to resume my concentration, I couldn't help thinking, 'This is what Tests are all about.' I lapped it all up and it was a great personal thrill to be part of such splendid bowling and the unique atmosphere of a Lord's Test.

England got their revenge in the next Test in which I officiated – at Leeds, when the ball turned square and Derek Underwood took 10 wickets in the match. The ball turned on the first morning because the groundsman had all sorts of problems preparing the wicket after recent thunderstorms – but the Aussies were 79–1 at lunch on the first day and then collapsed to 146 due to bad batting, rather than scintillating bowling by Underwood. They were demoralized early on, but to be fair the Aussies never moaned to the umpires — they made their official complaint to the ground authorities and were no trouble to us at any stage. They gave no quarter on the field, nor did they ask for any, and I respected Ian Chappell for sensible captaincy.

It was a difficult match to umpire because the ball was popping all over the place with close fielders hemming in the batsmen. The game was over by Saturday afternoon (the third day) and that's surely not right for a Test. But the fact remains that Test-class bowlers are expected to capitalize on a wicket that favours them, just as you expect a hundred from a class batsman when it's a flat wicket. That's what happened in 1972 at Leeds.

I enjoyed the 1972 Australians. Ian Chappell kept a tight rein on their behaviour, and although their batsmen all stood at the wicket, waiting to be given out, there were no complaints when the finger went up. Dennis Lillee looked a high-class fast bowler and their fielding — with Ross Edwards dominating one side and Paul Sheahan the other — was superb (always excluding poor old Bruce Francis!). It was a great personal thrill to stand twice in a series involving the Aussies. As a kid, you're brought up to believe that the Ashes games are the big ones, and at the end of the 1972 series I felt I was on the way as a Test umpire.

The following summer I stood in two Tests, and in the first, at Trent Bridge against the New Zealanders, I saw something I never expected — an England batsman giving himself out! It was Tony Lewis, to an appeal for a catch behind the wicket by Ken Wadsworth. All praise to Tony and no complaints from me about the other players' attitudes — but you just don't expect such actions in a Test!

England nearly came a cropper in that match against New Zealand — they won by just 38 runs after the Kiwis had been set 478 to win. But Trent Bridge is the only Test match ground in England where I would put the opposition in when I won the toss, because the pitch gets easier and easier as the game goes on. The Kiwis found this out and they gave England a fright —

although the home side were particularly generous in the matter of dropped catches. Two incidents involving Dennis Amiss stick in my mind from that Test — when he hit Bruce Taylor for four boundaries in a row and the bowler took out his white hankie and fluttered the sign of surrender, and, more significantly, when he was involved in a run-out with Geoff Boycott. Amiss sent Boycott back on the second run and he didn't make it. I believe this was the turning point in Dennis Amiss' Test career — before that he was in and out of the side and never really given the chance to establish himself. Here he was, having helped run out Boycott (not the fault of Amiss, I think), but he gritted his teeth, concentrated furiously and scored a century. He'd proved he had the right mental attitude for Test cricket by putting upsets behind him — and the next 12 months were prolific ones at Test level for Amiss.

My next Test that year was at the Oval where England were outplayed by a very strong West Indian side. What a batting line-up they had — Sobers at seven, Julien at eight and Boyce at nine, all playing shots as if there was no tomorrow! It was exhilarating stuff, especially with the high-spirited West Indian supporters. Unfortunately they got a little too enthusiastic when they rushed the field after Clive Lloyd reached his century. England's captain, Ray Illingworth, wasn't too happy at the protection given to the wicket, but I wasn't sure what he thought two umpires could do in the face of a couple of thousand! I was disturbed at these needless crowd invasions and felt the batsman should have been left alone to savour his moment of glory. Unfortunately, the Oval in 1973 was the forerunner of many regrettable crowd invasions throughout the seventies.

Frank Hayes scored 100 on his debut for England in that Test and I remember his knock for two reasons, apart from his dashing stroke-play. Before he'd scored, Gary Sobers deceived him with a beautiful slower ball. The ball pitched in the blockhole and it turned almost at right-angles down the leg side so Frank would never have been out lbw. Gary threw up his

arms and said, 'Ooh,' and Frank breathed again. He prospered and played very well on a turning wicket. In the final over of the day he hit the last two deliveries for 10 runs. They were off the slow left-armer, Inshan Ali, and they shot off like tracer bullets over mid-wicket.

This was a fine West Indian side. All but Inshan Ali had experience of county cricket and I could appreciate the point made plaintively by Alec Bedser, the England chairman of selectors. Big Alec pointed out that ten of the victorious West Indian team had perfected their skills in county cricket, and emphasized the fact that their good fortune was English cricket's loss, because the development of England cricketers was being retarded by overseas players. It was difficult to disagree with him.

*A rarity in Test cricket – a batsman actually walking for a catch behind the wicket before an umpire has to intervene. It's the 1973 Test between England and New Zealand at Trent Bridge. The bowler is Bruce Taylor, the keeper Ken Wadsworth, and the honest batsman saving me a little job is Tony Lewis. I wish there'd been more like Tony*

71

I stood in two Tests in 1974. The first marked Geoff Boycott's disappearance from Tests for three years. The Indian seam bowler, Solkar, got him out for the fourth time in five innings against his harmless left-arm away swing, so Boycott upped and left the Test scene. I think he was embarrassed and annoyed at getting out to such a mediocre trundler as Solkar — my theory was that 'Boycs' was playing too soon at the ball, rather than letting it come to him. 'Boycs' had learned to face the speed of Hall, Griffith, Pollock, Lillee and McKenzie and come through it with flying colours, yet here was this innocuous bowler making life difficult for him!

One other memory remains from that first Test against the Indians at Old Trafford. The Manchester weather lived up to its reputation and it was cold and rainy throughout. One day, just after the tea interval, it was getting rather dark and 'Dickie' Bird and I 'offered the light' to Gavaskar and Abid Ali. To our surprise Abid Ali said, 'No, thank you very much, I am playing well and I'd like to stay on.' Gavaskar just shrugged, even though it would have made sense to come off, because the Indians were simply trying to save the game. A couple of overs later Abid Ali had a slog at Underwood and Boycott took a great catch, running back from deep mid-wicket. The Indian tail was quickly rolled over, and afterwards the Indian captain, Wadekar, came to us and said in his best Peter Sellers-style accent, 'What am I to do about my batsmen? They won't come off when the light is bad.' Quite so, skipper.

My next Test in the summer of 1974 was a rain-affected draw, but not before the Pakistanis had kicked up a hell of a fuss about the way overnight rain had seeped under the covers and given Derek Underwood a wicket ideal for his skills. I felt sorry for the groundsman because the rain was so torrential that it got under the covers despite £10,000 worth of new equipment. The Pakistan manager complained that the rain had affected the wicket, but if their players had shown enough common sense they would never have needed to worry about saving the match. The patch that attracted Derek Underwood's attention wasn't really in the best place for him — it was just short of a length, outside the right-hander's leg stump, and he would have to bowl over the wicket to hit this patch, thereby ruling out much hope of lbws. But the Pakistan batsmen — most of them with county cricket experience — kept sweeping and 'gloving' the ball to the close fielders. Only Sarfraz — a bowler — played the right way. He stuck his left pad down the track and padded the ball away. He only scored a single but it took him a long time and he frustrated a great bowler in the process.

It was all faintly academic anyway, because rain on the last day washed out the Test, though not before I saw the greatest catch I've ever experienced. I was at the bowler's end when Wasim Raja lofted Underwood high to long-on. Tony Greig ran back, jumped and took the catch as he fell back towards the boundary ropes — a fantastically athletic effort, the kind of catch only a man of his height and anticipation could reach.

The world of politics and protest entered the Test arena the

*Leeds 1975 — and protest enters Test cricket. George Davis's supporters pour oil on the wicket and neither myself nor Tony Greig can believe it*

following summer when I stood in the first Test match that had ever been drawn because vandals dug up the wicket. Leeds 1975 will always be associated with George Davis and his supporters, who were so convinced that he was innocent that they dug up the Test wicket as proof. The feelings of the umpires and players can be imagined — what had we done to George Davis? Why should we be involved? The match was beautifully poised on that final day — there was bound to be a result and the Yorkshire folk were flocking towards Headingley with the same kind of anticipation we were all experiencing. I got a call from the ground just after nine o'clock, and when I saw the wicket I just couldn't believe the amount of oil that Davis's supporters had poured on to it. Fortunately it rained all day and the game would never have reached its expected gripping climax — but the thought nagged away at me for weeks: who would have the audacity to stop a Test match for reasons totally unconnected with cricket? I'd never heard of George Davis, but did his supporters have to ruin the innocent pleasures of others just to get him out of prison?

Apart from the attentions of the George Davis brigade, that Test was my first sight of England under Tony Greig's captaincy. He was certainly different from Mike Denness and Ray Illingworth, the two previous England captains I'd stood with as umpire — Greigy was more flamboyant and would try to lead from the front. But I honestly thought there was little between him and Mike Denness as tacticians — and Ray Illingworth left them both standing as an overall skipper. He could still be playing now if he felt like it, because he nursed himself towards the end and I felt he always had something left in reserve.

The Leeds Test marked the début of Phil Edmonds and he captured plenty of newspaper headlines for his bowling that was, in truth, fairly straightforward. The Aussies suffered a collective rush of blood to the head, tried to smash the young débutant out of sight, and Phil picked up 5 wickets. But what impressed me most about Edmonds was the way he fielded a scorching straight drive from Doug Walters off his own bowling.

It was an absolute screamer, yet Edmonds was down to it like a shot, picked it up and sauntered back to his mark. Not since Tony Lock had I seen an English bowler field like that to his own bowling, and I thought, 'Hello, this bloke can play a bit.' I don't think I was wrong — I like Edmonds' 'champagne' approach to cricket; he plays hard, but fairly and cheerfully, and he'll take a gamble. A fine all-round cricketer.

The year 1976 saw the arrival of that magnificent West Indies side with their superb fast bowlers and majestic batsmen. Their only weakness was their lack of a class spinner, but they didn't really need one with the pace attack of Roberts, Holding, Daniel and Holder. They scored their runs quickly enough to give the bowlers time to bowl out the opposition twice — the classic Test formula. Mind you, I think the 1979 West Indian side that won the Prudential World Cup was a better one, because Garner and Croft gave them even greater seam bowling penetration.

My first Test of that summer began in exciting fashion, but then it fizzled out into a disappointing draw. Underwood rattled the West Indians on the Friday, and with a full house at Lord's and the Tavern chorusing 'Rule Britannia' I was really enjoying the atmosphere. But it rained all day on the Saturday — it started just as we walked out at 11.25 and it just got heavier and heavier as the day progressed. It was so disappointing to see a huge crowd being turned away, especially in a season of almost unrelieved sunshine. Come the last day and the West Indies were setting themselves up for a crack at the total set by Tony Greig; they needed 7 an over off the last 20 overs, with plenty of wickets in hand. However once the final onslaught started they lost a few wickets and called off the chase. But Tony Greig wanted to carry on in the vain hope that he could snatch a victory. I was a little annoyed because there was no hope of either side winning and it was just bloody-mindedness on the part of both captains. Greigy had upset the West Indians with his remarks that he hoped to make them grovel, and they always bowled twice as quickly to him that summer whenever he came in to bat. But in turn Greigy gave them no quarter — and at Lord's the result was a rather sour stalemate.

My next Test that summer was happily rather different. Leeds on the first day was the best day's cricket I can ever remember. The wicket was hard, fast and bouncy, with something in it for batsmen and bowlers. At lunch the West Indies were 147–0 and Greenidge and Fredericks — who both got centuries — put on 192 for the first wicket. Viv Richards and Lawrence Rowe scored rapid fifties and the West Indians reached 437/9 by the close. Magnificent stuff — I recall thinking to myself, 'This is what cricket is all about', as the ball disappeared into the crowd. England lost that Test but not without a great fight by Tony Greig who battled all the way, putting on nearly 200 with Alan Knott and swinging the bat in the second knock when the game was slipping away from England. In that second innings he put on 46 with Alan Ward — and Alan didn't even get a run! I remember reprimanding Viv Richards for trying to run the game from his position at gully — Andy Roberts appealed for lbw against Peter Willey and Viv started dancing around in the gully. I said 'Not out' and had a few words with the West Indian skipper, Clive Lloyd, about some volatile appeals! Another memory from that Test — the press made a lot out of the fact that both umpires went to point, rather than square leg, when Andy Roberts was bowling. The newshounds suspected a throwing controversy, even though I made a point of gesticulating towards the sun. I really couldn't focus properly from square leg because of the bright sun that was such a feature of that summer — but things were misconstrued.

I saw the 1977 Australians at first hand in a couple of Tests — and they were easily the worst outfit I've seen wearing the famous green caps. Their batting relied almost entirely on Greg Chappell; there were too many chancy players in the side. I felt sorry for Chappell because he couldn't be expected to bat at both ends. The fielding had declined since the era of Edwards, Sheahan, Mallett and Ian Chappell, and the bowling wasn't all that special, either. But would England have dominated the series if Rick McCosker had caught Geoff Boycott early in his innings at Trent Bridge? And where would Boycott have been without the dashing example of Alan Knott at the other end? Imponderables, I agree, and there's no doubt that England were better led and better organized in that series — but slender things like a dropped catch or a great innings can transform a series.

The last Test of that 1977 series was a bad one for me. I think I let the public down because I didn't really concentrate as much as I should. I was still in a state of shock over the Packer affair and I couldn't believe that I was standing in the last authentic Test between those two great rivals, England and Australia. So many top-class players had signed for Packer that it looked as if the very life-blood of cricket had been sucked away. My old Kent team-mates Derek Underwood, Alan Knott and Bob Woolmer were due to fly out to World Series cricket that winter. So was Tony Greig, a man who'd done much for English cricket, no matter what his detractors might say. I was in a bit of a daze and kept wondering if this was to be the end of the kind of Test cricket we'd all been brought up to revere. I wasn't as vigilant or as attentive as I should have been and I don't think I really earned my money in that match. I didn't blame anyone for the decisions taken, but with the threat of bans from first-class cricket facing all the Packer players I feared the worst. I honestly thought I'd never see them playing Tests again, and at the end of the drawn match I said to the Kent lads I'd known since we were youngsters, 'All the best, Derek, Alan, Bob — regards to the families, I hope we'll see each other again soon on the field of play.' It felt like the end of an era.

Mike Brearley held the England side together well in that climactic series, but there were deep divisions in the Australian party. Craig Serjeant — a non-Packer man — lost his batting place to the reserve keeper, Richie Robinson, even though Serjeant scored 81 in his first Test at Lord's! Kim Hughes, who quite frankly wasn't good enough for World Series cricket at the time, was included in the last Test at the Oval simply because nobody else was any more competent. Overall it was an unhappy occasion, and I'm delighted my initial instincts proved unfounded.

I stood in a couple of Tests the following year — and my outstanding memory is the swing bowling at Lord's of Ian Botham. He also scored a century, a typically ferocious, majestic knock, but his swing bowling reminded me of Bob Massie six years earlier. He's a great lad to handle, with bags of confidence and the ability to relax and enjoy a joke on the field as well. He's box-office potential, I'm sure, and he can be a force in the game for years to come. His wry sense of humour was revealed on that Monday morning when he ran through the Pakistanis with a devastatingly controlled display of bowling. It was difficult for both umpire and bowler to gauge the extent of the swing that morning, and when I turned down an lbw appeal against Iqbal Qasim he turned round and said, 'Doing too much, wasn't it?' I agreed. The next ball knocked out two stumps — and Botham turned round and grinned, 'That's out, isn't it?' A real trier, he loves his cricket and he's the kind of cricketer you hope will prosper because he gives a lot of pleasure to many.

One pleasing decision from me in that Lord's Test — I almost gave Haroon Rashid out, caught behind the wicket, when I realized that the only man who was appealing was the bowler, Ian Botham. Bob Taylor and the slips stayed down and my instinct told me things weren't quite right. On the TV action replay that night I saw that Haroon was about a foot away from the ball. Thank you again, Auntie Beeb.

Some thoughts on the 1978 New Zealanders — I stood in the Test at the Oval where David Gower got his first Test century, following in the footsteps of other great Leicestershire left-hand batsmen like Clive Inman and . . . David Constant! One incident in this Test made me realize how amateur the Kiwis are — as Mike Brearley sprinted for a quick single, the throw from Mark Burgess hit his bat and careered off for a couple of overthrows.

Robert Anderson — a genial soul off the field — shouted, 'Hey, ref, they can't do that, can they?' I'm afraid they could, and I was amazed at the gap in his cricketing knowledge. Things like that are part and parcel of an English pro's game, and we tend to forget that tourists like the New Zealanders are essentially amateurs. Men like Geoff Howarth, Glenn Turner, John Parker and Richard Hadlee may have become better players in the county game over here, but they're still in the minority among New Zealand sides. Individually, any New Zealand touring side is almost entirely made up of charming blokes, but they still lack a little bit of cricket professionalism, although I'm glad to say they are making impressive strides.

I stood in two Tests involving the 1979 Indians and the second one, at the Oval, was one of the best in my experience. Thanks to a superb double hundred by Gavaskar, they came within a few runs of snatching a famous victory on a slow Oval wicket. I still think the Indians should have sent out Viswanath to partner Gavaskar when the match was there for the taking. Instead Kapil Dev played the same way that he would have played a few overs later and slogged the ball to long-on for 0. If it was up to me I'd always trust a stroke player, and at the time there were enough overs in hand for Viswanath to play himself in and then launch the attack. After all, he's one of the best batsmen in the world. In the end, Peter Willey saved England by bowling his off-breaks very tightly to a one-day field and containing the Indians. I think this was probably the match that made up Mike Brearley's mind to take Derek Underwood on the trip to Australia. Phil Edmonds, for some reason, didn't bowl all that tightly and I'm sure Brearley must have longed for Underwood's control and meanness at some stage on that long final day.

So many memories from my Tests — and I hope there are just as many to come. Sadly, the test that should have been the highlight of my career only served to magnify a dilemma that faces umpires — when to resume play after rain. On the Saturday of the Centenary Test, Dickie Bird and I were under great pressure to start play in conditions that just weren't playable. People kept saying, 'This is a one-off match, can't you forget the lawbook!' Well, at no stage before the Test were we told to treat it as anything other than a Test and, as far as we were concerned, we had to be consistent.

The criteria for resumption of play are: can the batsman stand or run freely between the wickets; can the bowler run up with freedom; and if the fielders within about thirty yards of the bat have reasonably free movement. All umpires have received instructions in recent years but play should always take place whenever reasonable and obviously we wanted to get going as soon as possible, but you just can't bend the laws for one game. The captains — Ian Botham and Greg Chappell — and all the players agreed with our judgment, and a slight injury to Geoff Boycott proved our point. When we managed to start on that Saturday afternoon, Boycott slipped on a wet part of the square and strained his leg. On the Monday, he fielded at slip because his leg was still sore . . .

# 6 The Humour of the Game

I know that top-class cricket is now a serious game and getting more so — but some lovely moments still take place out there in the middle that the spectators miss. Thankfully there's still time for a laugh and a joke, but the umpire must never be seen to start the fun, in my opinion. He should be slightly apart from it, but can still enjoy the humour in a quiet, unobtrusive way.

Obviously there are fewer laughs to be had in Test matches. They are the acme of the game and I find that everyone is so busy concentrating that there's little time for humour, or for that matter much chat at all. But it's funny how humour can be found even in the tensest moments. There was that great Test at the Oval when India, set 438 to win by Mike Brearley, came within 9 runs of a famous victory with just 2 wickets left. The hero of their innings was that lovely little fellow Sunil Gavaskar, and on the Monday, as the England innings drew to a close, he asked me as I stood at square leg, 'How many do you think they'll leave us?'

I said, 'Oh, about 420.'

'Do you think we'll get them?' he asked.

I said, 'If you do, someone will have to get a double hundred', and we both laughed.

The next day, as he reached his 200, with the match in India's pocket, I leaned over to him as he acknowledged the applause and whispered, 'You didn't have to take me literally, you know!' and he enjoyed the joke.

*Three incidents involving me which prove that the world of international cricket isn't always tense and exacting. In the first (above) I count out the exhausted Clive Lloyd after the strain of all those quick singles had got to him.*

I've known some lovely moments in county cricket and many of them involve Essex, who are a joy to play against and to umpire. Ever since I've been involved in the game Essex have had a reputation as a talented, humorous bunch, and a lot of the credit for that must go to their former captain, Brian 'Tonker' Taylor. 'Tonker' was a real old-style sergeant-major but he had a heart of gold; he could see the funny side of things and his players would do anything for him. One day at Derby

Keith Pont took the mickey out of 'Tonker'. The skipper had
Ponty fielding third man in one over and fine leg the next — and
on the large Derby ground that meant quite a walk between
overs. Well, Ponty spotted a bike beside the boundary and he
was next seen cycling the distance between the overs! It
brought the house down and 'Tonker' could see the joke. Then
there was the 1971 match at Colchester between Essex and the
Indian tourists. Stuart Turner was caught up in a terrific traffic

*Then (above left)
I find a sensible place
to park a fielder's
crash helmet. And
finally (above right)
England's Peter
Willey helps me
complete my leg-bye
signal after I'd
stumbled in the first
attempt.*

83

jam, arrived late and was made twelfth man. Essex had to field first and Stuart settled down to a nice spot of sunbathing in the players' enclosure. Now 'Tonker', being a strict disciplinarian, would want his twelfth man to be available at all times on behalf of the captain, and the Essex lads knew this. They spotted Stuart dozing off before 'Tonker' did, and a few of them set the skipper up. 'Hey, Tonker,' they said, 'have you seen Stuart over there?'

He looked over and in his deepest, gruffest sergeant-major's voice barked out, 'Stuart!!' And Stuart promptly fell out of his deckchair in fright.

A great character was 'Tonker' Taylor — he gave his lads discipline but also the ability to laugh at life. Essex will, I hope, always stay the same, with Ray East doing his marvellous Ministry of Silly Walks routine as he comes on to the field and John Lever doing his best to knock my hat off as he runs in to bowl. . . .

Another amusing incident early in my umpiring career came when Stewart Storey, the Surrey all-rounder, pulled the leg of the Derbyshire secretary, Major Carr. Stewart was batting when he complained to me about the dazzling floral tie worn by some bloke standing beside the sightscreen behind the bowler's arm. I had to go and ask him to move away and as I got near I was horrified to see that it was being worn by the home county's secretary! Anyway, I did my duty and afterwards Major Carr apologised fulsomely to Stewart, who was trying hard not to grin. After all, it's not every day you manage to set up the umpire and a county secretary with one little jape!

Derek Randall is one player I always cite whenever people lament the dearth of 'characters' in the modern game. Derek simply loves his cricket and never seems bored. He's always keyed up, chattering away to himself and playing imaginary shots as he stands in the covers between deliveries. He's a magnificent fielder, but wasn't always so reliable. In his early days with Nottinghamshire you didn't really know where the ball was going when he had it in his hand. One such match involved

84

Hampshire, when I umpired. Mike Hill, Hampshire's reserve keeper, pushed a ball for a single and decided on a second. Derek went for a spectacular throw but the ball lollipopped high in the air . . . at the same time Mike Hill fell over halfway up the second run. He had to scramble home on his hands and knees while the ball was still miles up in the air. Derek's skipper, Mike Smedley, wasn't very amused but the rest of us were in stitches. Bob White had to bowl three more deliveries to finish his over and the pair of us were giggling so much that I don't know what would have happened if the ball had hit the pad! I could hardly see for laughing, especially whenever I looked at young Derek's sheepish face!

Tony Greig was another great character with a wry sense of humour that some people mistook for gamesmanship. Often he'd lead the team out and, in earshot of me, he'd shout, 'Right lads, no appealing unless it's out.' In other words, if Greigy and Co. appealed, the umpire should understand it was bound to be very close — which anybody who knows Greigy realizes wasn't always the case. But he'd make the remark to his team with a smile on his face and a wink, and it was impossible not to be amused by a player whom I always found basically fair and good company.

Brian Close was another amazing man. I've never seen anybody show less pain when suffering from a blow that would have flattened most men. I've umpired matches in which blood has seeped through his boot after he was hit, yet he wouldn't say a thing and refused to go off. Once, in a match at Weston-super-Mare, Lancashire's Harry Pilling swept Brian Langford's off-break off the full meat of the bat — right into Close's kidneys. At that time, Langford had just lost the Somerset captaincy in favour of the hard man from Yorkshire, and naturally Langford was concerned that nobody should think he was indifferent to Close's injury in case there was a suspicion of sour grapes about the new appointment. So Brian rushed down the wicket, saying, 'Are you all right, skipper, are you all right?'

Close replied, 'Where did it hit me?' while all the close fielders winced at the blow and noticed that the ball had ended up at mid-wicket.

One of the real characters in my time was Tony Lock. He skippered me at Leicester and set an amazing example of enthusiasm and dedication. But sometimes that enthusiasm went too far and we weren't too keen on all the kissing and hugging at every fall of an opposition wicket. This was a new fad that Locky had brought back from his successful stint in Australia's Sheffield Shield competitions and the grizzled, hard-bitten old pros gave him a few funny looks when he tried it on at Grace Road. Life went on rather uneasily for a couple of weeks under the new intimate regime until Peter Marner sorted out Locky. He caught one at slip off Locky's bowling, and when he saw the skipper running down the wicket with lips pursed he dropped the ball and ran off towards the sightscreen! In the next match one of the Leicestershire lads dropped a catch that would have given Locky a hat-trick. When the unfortunate fieldsman was harangued by Locky, he told him, 'I didn't catch it because I couldn't face another of your kisses!' Locky got the point after that.

But he was marvellous value and a great competitor on his dodgy knees. Once, at Grace Road, he misfielded rather badly for a player of his brilliance. The ball hit a divot and went through his legs, and he was barracked by three spectators sitting on the same bench. Locky went purple in the face, stuck up his hand and commanded, 'Stop the game.' He walked slowly over to the trio of barrackers. 'Was that you?' he demanded three times. On each occasion the answer was, 'No.' Unabashed, Locky declared, 'Any more of that and I'll come over and pan you.' Then he turned round magisterially and commanded us, 'Carry on with the game!' The amazing thing was that Locky couldn't understand why we were all doubled up with laughter. . . .

My old Kent colleague Peter Richardson was one of the great practical jokers of my time. I remember when Mike Denness first came down from Scotland via Ayr Academy. Peter got the local press into the dressing-room and, as acting skipper, gave them a cock-and-bull tale about Denness coming from the wilds of Banffshire and that he was a sheep farmer! The next day the press was full of the story of the backwoodsman from Banffshire playing the Englishman's game.

Then there was the time he pinched some letter-heading from Lord's to play a joke on Kent's off-spinner, Colin Page. This was at the time of the throwing controversy, when the finger of suspicion was being pointed even at the most immaculate of bowlers. Colin certainly came into that category, but Peter sent him an official-looking letter from Lord's which said they were concerned about the legality of his bowling action and that they'd be having a look at him again shortly! Poor old Colin walked about for several days with a face like a wet weekend, and in the end we had to put him out of his misery. He admitted the incident had helped him lose weight.

Who else but quick-thinking Peter Richardson would come up with a crack as he walked off after being dismissed in one of the early John Player League matches that were televized? In those days there was always an interviewer on hand to ask the batsman about his dismissal as he walked into the pavilion. 'Tell me, Peter,' said the BBC man, 'what kind of ball was it that got you?' Came the reply, 'A Stuart Surridge!'

There have been a few umpires around who were larger than life. My father-in-law, George Lambert, used to be an opening bowler with Gloucestershire and he's regaled me with some great stories about Frank Chester. Frank had a ready wit and appreciated a joke against himself. One day my father-in-law came into bat, still rather hung-over from the previous night's drinking. 'What do you want?' shouted Frank from the umpire's end as George deliberated over his guard. 'Gin and tonic,' he shouted back, and Frank grinned from ear to ear. Then there was the time that Frank won a few bob off George in a snooker match. Now Frank had lost an arm in the First World War and, to be honest, George was rather embarrassed when Frank challenged him to a game of snooker in a Manchester hotel after a long day in the field. They agreed to play half-a-crown a game and George was still feeling rather sorry for Frank and wondering if he could possibly take his money off him when Frank whipped out a special arm rest and proceeded to thrash George out of sight for the rest of the evening!

I'm glad to say there's still a bit of community spirit in the county game and it's always lovely for me to meet and share a joke with players whom I met when I was a county cricketer. But I make sure I keep my distance on the field, because it's important for the umpire to feel apart from the leg-pulling unless he's directly involved. We umpires all like a laugh, though, and there's no shortage of 'characters' in white coats. 'Dickie' Bird, a man who loves the game deeply, likes nothing better than to chat about old times ('Eeh, David, we could murder this bowling,' he'll tell me at an interval). There's Bill Alley, who's always got a story to tell out of the corner of his mouth — 'Oyster Bill', he's nicknamed, because his mouth is always opening and closing! Cec Pepper was a real card, a larger-than-life Aussie who used to take himself off to greyhound meetings whenever possible. He'd turn up the next day, bemoaning his fate at the hands of the bookies or telling us about this three-legged dog that let him down.

My advice to the club umpire, if he's tempted to join in the banter on the field, is to resist the temptation until it's clear that the players want you involved as well. Obviously if you fall flat on your face and everybody laughs, enjoy the fun, but don't initiate the conversations. Have a natter at square leg but wait until the fielder talks to you. He may be a bowler who's trying to work out his next over in his mind or looking for signs of weakness in the batsman, or he may be the opening bat who's getting his mind attuned to the start of his side's innings. Concentrate on the game rather than the next quip, and you'll find that cricketers — a very friendly bunch in general — won't leave you out of the chat. But beware of being intrusive, and don't get on the players' nerves with incessant chatter. Fundamentally, you're there to supervise the game, rather than to say, 'Did you hear the one about. . . ?'

# 7 The Great Players

I've been privileged to have a close-up view of most of the world's best players in the last decade. Although an umpire has to concentrate on every ball and put personal considerations to one side, he can still appreciate high skill when he sees it. Umpires are no different from players in that they talk about the great innings they've seen, which player is on his way to the top, and which bowler has added another element to his bowling repertoire. We've all got ideas on how the game should be played and we all like to pick our best-ever side to play Mars on a good wicket. I'm no different. . . .

The ideal Test side must have balance. The batting must comprise various qualities and the bowling should also be varied. There's no point in having four fast bowlers, in my opinion; if three can't do the job I don't see that an extra one makes all that difference. So you must have a couple of spinners in the side. You must also pick the best wicket-keeper; nobody expects world-class fast bowlers to bat, so why ask the same of a keeper, who's also in a specialist position? If he can bat, that's a bonus, but it's not crucial.

Right, here's my World XI for a Test match, based on the players I've seen. It's in batting order:

| | |
|---|---|
| Sunil Gavaskar | Alan Knott |
| Geoff Boycott | Dennis Lillee |
| Rohan Kanhai | Michael Holding |
| Viv Richards | Derek Underwood |
| Gary Sobers | Erapalli Prasanna |
| Clive Lloyd (Captain) | |

## SUNIL GAVASKAR

He's played brilliantly over the years for a Test side not renowned for its batting, and he's shouldered the responsibilities with calm assurance. In a fine player, I always look to see if he plays through the V — that area between mid-off and mid-on. Sunil plays immaculately straight through that line, and on the rare occasions when he plays a loose shot he'll cup his hands to the side of his eyes and look straight down the wicket. That's his way of telling himself to keep playing through the V, and you can bet he won't play another loose shot across the line for an hour or so.

For a small man he's very muscular and strong, and hits very hard off both back and front foot. His concentration is faultless; that double hundred at the Oval against Mike Brearley's England side was magnificent. The wicket was low and slow — not ideal batting conditions — and he knew he first had to save the game for India. Then he tightened the screw and upped the tempo. In the end, fatigue got him out.

Gavaskar is a philosophical character with the ideal Test match temperament. Nothing gets him worked up on the field — he didn't even bat an eyelid when John Snow barged him over in that famous incident at Lord's.

## GEOFF BOYCOTT

It's fashionable to criticize Boycott for slow scoring but those critics miss the point that an opening batsman's fundamental task is to see off the new ball attack and then, if possible, build from there. Nobody in my time has been better equipped to play that role than Boycott. A Test side needs at least one of his type — you can't have all your batsmen going out and throwing the bat at the ball. He has the technique, the judgment and the mental strength to see the shine off — and he has more strokes than many people realize, particularly the back-foot drive through the covers, his favourite shot.

## ROHAN KANHAI

I think the number three position is the most important one. He must be able to attack or defend in the appropriate conditions. Rohan could do either and he was the best all-round batsman I've seen. He could be brilliant or play a long innings for the side — he had West Indian flair harnessed to the professionalism of an England pro. It's more difficult to pick the right ball to hit than to flash the bat at everything, and over the years Rohan learned his trade with Warwickshire and became the best man I've seen at picking the right ball to hit.

## VIV RICHARDS

When he's in the mood, nobody can bowl to this chap. An hour from him is enough to win a match, but I'd like to see him have to get his head down and bat for more than four hours. Where Rohan Kanhai could bat all day and put the game beyond the opposition's reach, Viv gets fed up after a while and chances his arm. But he must have shown a new maturity to play so many superb innings with his bad back injury in Australia. Time will tell if he matures into a Kanhai, but I doubt it — I think he hits across his front leg too much, and when his eye dims and he gets a bit older he may get caught in the slips a lot, playing across the line. He's a remarkable on-side player, and nobody I've seen picks up the line of the ball more quickly.

## GARY SOBERS

I always felt a magnificent player like Sobers was wasted at number six, even though he obviously needed a rest after his bowling exertions. He's simply the best all-rounder ever, and the fact that he played to such a standard for a continuous 20 years all round the world is remarkable. He could field anywhere, he could be as quick as anybody with the new ball, he had the ability to run the ball into the right-hander (a deadly ball, that one), and although I never really rated his spinning, he could still winkle out a few when the heat was on. And what a batsman! He hit everything straight, and the way he'd crack the bowler straight down the wicket off the back foot showed his class. He had a terrific eye and was one of the hardest hitters I've ever seen.

Gary played cricket like the man he was — he'd take a chance and try to keep the game flowing. He's a generous, sunny man and I'll be lucky if I see another cricketer like Gary Sobers in my lifetime.


## CLIVE LLOYD

I've made him captain because I think he's the phlegmatic type best suited to the task. He doesn't panic and I think he learned a lot about captaincy from studying Lancashire's Jackie Bond for several seasons. A gentleman, he never gives the umpire any trouble.

He's the hardest hitter of a ball in my experience, and coming in at number six he would be in a position to demoralize the bowlers. I think they'd just have to bowl line and length at him and hope he has an off-day. He's a brilliant fielder, and since all my side are judged to be in their prime I would have him in the covers dominating his side of the field, with no worries about knee operations on his mind.


## ALAN KNOTT

In my opinion, the greatest wicket-keeper ever. He set a remarkable standard for so long that anything slightly less than immaculate stood out. Bob Taylor, a superb keeper, was unlucky to be around at the same time, but Knotty had that little bit extra. He always kept me on my toes because just when you're thinking, 'That snick's going wide, better get ready to signal 4 runs,' he'd pop up and get a glove to the ball.

As a batsman he saved England on countless occasions, and

I'll never forget the way he galvanized Geoff Boycott at Trent Bridge in 1977 against the Aussies. England were really in trouble but Knotty came in and took the fight to the bowlers. It looked a different game from then on, and Boycott also looked a different batsman. Knotty worked out his own method to play the quickies, and his footwork and temperament were tremendous.

## DENNIS LILLEE

Hostile and subtle, he always believed he was about to get somebody out. A lot of fast bowlers can manage a quick, sharp burst and that's them finished for the day, but Lillee could always come back and bowl superbly for long periods. He fought back magnificently after some bad injuries, and those lay-offs gave him time to think about his craft. He would come back an even better bowler because he'd realized there are other ways of getting a batsman out than by sheer pace. He could do such a lot with the ball — both through the air and off the wicket.

A lot has been said about his temperament but I never really had any trouble with him. He needed a fellow like Ian Chappell to crack down on any histrionics and I believe trouble arises with Lillee only if he suspects the umpire is incompetent. That's why he never had any real complaints in England.

## MICHAEL HOLDING

A Rolls-Royce among fast bowlers — and I'm sure he's got something left under the bonnet as he cruises in. A magnificent sight, a beautifully fluid, elegant mover — and such pace through the air! In 1976 at the Oval he showed true greatness. It was a flat, slow wicket, yet Holding clean bowled eight England batsmen by sheer speed through the air. He gets a lot of lift from the slowest of wickets because of his lithe action, and although he's had temperamental problems abroad I've never had any complaints about him in England. He seems a nice, quiet lad who just gets on with his job.

## DEREK UNDERWOOD

A unique bowler who will bowl out a side on a wicket giving him just a little help — and if it's a flat one, he'll keep one end shored up while the quick bowlers take a breather. When the wicket is wet, the first bowler you put on is Underwood; the ball will turn and lift and he'll be virtually unplayable. On these wickets he gets a lot of batsmen out caught off their gloves because they just can't get out of the way in time — he's too quick. He never seems to bother that so much is expected of him when the wicket's in his favour — other bowlers would buckle under the strain of being expected to deliver the goods, but Derek hasn't failed too many times when everything's set up for him.

A terrific trier, he hates bowling a bad ball. I played in Kent Seconds with him and he's still the same serious-minded, conscientious, modest chap.

## ERAPALLI PRASANNA

Many people will be surprised at my choice of off-spinner, but he was the biggest spinner of the off-break I've seen and he could flight it beautifully. That 1971 Indian side with their four great slow bowlers — Bedi, Chandra, Venkat and Prasanna — were a delight to watch, unless you were the umpire concentrating furiously at the bowler's end, and the best in my opinion was Prasanna. He had all the usual Indian guile and patience and he didn't mind the batsman getting after him. On a good wicket, where skill and unflappability are needed to dismiss good batsmen, Prasanna is my man. His only weakness is that he can't bat or field all that well, but I'll find a safe place for him in the field.

94

I reckon I've got five all-time greats in my side — Kanhai, Sobers, Knott, Underwood and Lillee. I only have to hide one player in the field — Prasanna. I've got the best wicket-keeper ever, and magnificent fieldsmen like Lloyd, Sobers and Richards. Boycott's also a fine fielder and Kanhai didn't miss many at first slip.

If I had to pick my best one-day side, I'd obviously tinker around with this line-up. A one-day side needs great players who can get on with it a little more, so Boycott and Gavaskar have to make way. And you need good fielders as well. Here's my team:

| | |
|---|---|
| John Jameson | Alan Knott |
| Gordon Greenidge | Ray Illingworth (Captain) |
| Rohan Kanhai | Derek Underwood |
| Viv Richards | Dennis Lillee |
| Gary Sobers | Andy Roberts |
| Clive Lloyd | |

Four changes, then:

## JOHN JAMESON

I think Jameson should have played more times for England. I'd love to have seen him take on the Australian and West Indian fast bowlers who made life so difficult for the English batsmen in the mid-seventies. Only Tony Greig really stood up to the quickies and took them on at that time, and Jameson was brave and had a magnificent eye. If you pitched them short he'd hook you out of sight, and he wouldn't be found hanging his bat out to dry and get caught in the slips. It was a great loss to the game when he retired early — an obvious loss to the spectators but also to the players and umpires, because he was a charming, sporting, uncomplaining person.

## GORDON GREENIDGE

I think this chap could become a better player than Viv Richards. He's technically more correct, having played a lot longer in England, and he gives the ball a hell of a crack. Aggressive, powerful and dominant, he and Jameson would either get the innings off to a flying start or get out — but if they *do* fail, at least they won't have used up too many overs.

## RAY ILLINGWORTH

This great tactician would captain the side, and, because I'm the manager, he would bowl a lot too! A one-day side has to be prepared for all eventualities and Illy's bowling would be invaluable — canny, mean and subtle, he bowled such a good line and length. He used to bowl so close to the stumps that his arm would come over the non-striker's leg stump in line with the striker's off stump, so that the batsman was usually out if he missed the ball. But he could use the crease if the ball was turning too much and he was a past-master at cutting down the amount of turn.

As a batsman he could fiddle and nudge his way to some handy runs, and his calm temperament was ideal for the kind of tight finishes you get in limited-over matches.

Illy is the obvious captain — he's forgotten more about the game than many others know. The way he held that England side together for a few seasons, papering over the cracks and waiting for the moment to strike to pinch a victory, was superb.

## ANDY ROBERTS

He gets my vote over Holding because he bowls a better line and length. Because he bowls so straight, he never gives the batsman room to step back from the stumps and improvise. His bouncer is superb — it comes straight at the batsman and can be really unsettling. Too many fast bowlers waste their energies by bowling tennis ball-type bouncers. Not Roberts — when he lets one go, it's heading straight for the batsman.

In the field Lloyd, Sobers, Richards and Greenidge are superb, and because I would want Illingworth to attack all the time I would have Jameson, Kanhai and the captain himself close up to the wickets throughout. Too many limited-over games are lost by shutting up shop in the field and trying to keep the batsmen in. With my varied bowling attack, I'd expect to dismiss the opposition by attacking cricket.

# 8 The Future of Cricket

For nearly 20 years I've been part of first-class cricket in England, and as each season passes I read and hear that the game isn't what it used to be. Is anything? It's fashionable to lament the passing of institutions, conventions and respect for authority, and to some extent cricket has lost some of its attractions, but I sincerely feel that its more enduring qualities are still there.

I think the mix of competitions is just about right in England. The county clubs need the cash from limited-over competitions and the players therefore can't really complain that there's too much cricket. I hope that the amount of three-day cricket is never restricted, because this is the way that players learn to develop into Test cricketers. In Tests, it's not enough for a player to bowl line and length to a defensive field, and a batsman can't go in and start slogging all around him within a few overs. Test cricket is a long, patient game that takes its toll of players both mentally and physically, and the education for that process is provided by county cricket.

A batsman must have enough innings in a season to develop his technique. The more times he goes to the wicket the more chance he's got of working out his game. I hear about proposals to limit the number of county matches and to substitute, say, 16 four-day games instead. That will drastically cut down the amount of experience a young batsman can gain in a season. I'd like to see more three-day games if possible. I don't think there's too much cricket, and if the season could be extended a little into the usually sunny month of September there'd be no complaints from me, because I think it would benefit English cricketers — and after all, a fair amount of revenue from Test cricket in England is ploughed back to the counties, so it's in the counties' interests to have a strong England side. The more success enjoyed by England's Test team, the more people will come and watch.

I don't think the overseas players have generally helped England's Test prospects over the years. Of course, it's been thrilling to see such great players in the county championship, but there was a stage when there were too many of them. The overseas players were dominating the key batting positions and the young English lads were getting no chance to learn consistently about batting in the middle. Look how long Bob Woolmer languished down the order with Kent before he got the chance to stake a place for England from a more advantageous batting position. I think the regulations that will limit the amount of overseas players per county are very sound, and in the end will benefit England. No one wants to lose the chance of seeing great players, but there have been a few mediocre overseas players in the county championship in my time. The counties would have been better advised to bring on a young English player instead of paying big money for a chap who didn't deliver the goods.

There's nothing radically wrong with the game in England as I see it. There's a little petty gamesmanship now and again, and no umpire likes that, but in the long run the real responsibility lies with the captains. I believe the captain is responsible for the way cricket is played at any level. If both captains want a good game of cricket, you'll get one. If one of them has a bee in his bonnet or is feeling unco-operative, the game will suffer. I believe a cricketer should conduct himself with decorum and be a good ambassador for his club side, his county and his country, but unless he has a strong captain to keep him in line and encourage him to behave maturely, examples of bad sportsmanship and aggro will still be seen.

I'm more worried in behavioural terms about Tests abroad. Make no mistake about it, the kids all over the world copy their idols in mannerisms as well as attempted skills, and the more times we see bowlers kicking over stumps and running into umpires, and batsmen refusing to walk, the worse for the game in the long run. Several famous Test players lack self-discipline and it's up to the individual boards of control to say, 'Pull yourselves together.' I suppose World Series Cricket has some responsibility for this decline in behaviour on the field. That type of cricket was geared to action, to aggression, to a few carefully staged bits of aggro to entertain crowds that hadn't just turned up to watch the cricket. But now that Packer cricket no longer exists, it's surely time to get back to the kind of standards that helped make the Packer players into world-class cricketers.

I have no real criticism of Kerry Packer, though. He taught us all how to sell the game through the media, advertising and sponsorship. Indirectly, he made many people realize how little the English county player was being paid — and to the players whom he signed he must have seemed like Father Christmas. But I think the English players who signed for World Series cricket must have missed the atmosphere of Test cricket, particularly the Kent lads I knew so well. I remember standing beside Alan Knott as he acknowledged the applause of the Trent Bridge crowd for his great century against the Aussies in 1977. The cheering, the ovation, the atmosphere — it was fantastically heart-warming. I said to Knotty, 'Don't tell me you're going to give up all this for Packer.' He smiled and told me it was the money.

I had an offer to go to Australia and stand in the World Series matches. I turned it down, not for patriotic reasons but because I didn't think it was enough. Just after the final Oval Test in 1977 Richie Benaud rang me up and offered me £8,000 to sign. I refused because that was half of what some Packer players were getting, and as chairman of the first-class umpires and a prime activist for umpires to get the same money as the players

OPPOSITE *Dennis Lillee here makes the kind of extravagant appeal that's been popularized by World Series Cricket; the fans who don't care all that much about the game love to see such histrionics, while the poor old umpire faces even more pressure*

I would have been wrong to desert my principles just for the sake of a few thousand quid. I told Richie that, if I could have the same amount as the lesser Packer players (about £16,000), I'd sign. I had no qualms about considering the offer because I wasn't like the England players since I wasn't thumbing my nose at the Establishment. During the winter I don't do any umpiring, so I don't see why I would be unpatriotic to go to Australia and be back in the spring, ready for another English season. I wasn't refusing to get involved in a Test during the winter, unlike the Test players who signed for Packer. Anyway, it was all hypothetical, because Richie never did come back with another offer!

I'd like to have gone to Australia, if only to take a look at the umpiring standards over there. Everyone tells me the English first-class umpires are the best, but we are involved in so much cricket that we *should* be. Umpires are like batsmen — the more they play, the better they get, so the more times an umpire gets involved with pressure, the better he becomes, because he grows in experience. If you're only standing in a few big matches per season you've got little chance of improving. Also the bounce is different in Australia, and more tricky for the umpire to judge as the ball comes through at chest height. That's when you get slight deflections and you have to be very vigilant to spot them.

Many players tell me that the international game needs a panel of top umpires who would fly around the world officiating in Tests, as in international soccer. It sounds good in theory, but from what the Test players tell me, that panel would be composed of almost entirely English umpires. I honestly can't see other countries standing for an 'international' panel of English umpires — I think the whole idea is only attractive as a hypothesis. It would be better if more effort was made to lift the standards of the umpires in the particular countries. I think the idea of exchanging umpires is a good one — it was tried to a certain extent in England in the late seventies and I'd be happy to be involved in an exchange visit. It's all experience for the job, after all.

I'm very optimistic about the continuing good standard of English umpiring in first-class cricket. There was a time when not enough young candidates were coming through, presumably because the money didn't seem all that attractive. But now several former county players are applying because they can see a reasonably secure financial future in umpiring — and that's bound to mean the standards will be kept high. I've been chairman of the first-class umpires group since 1977 and Alan Whitehead, David Evans and Arthur Jepson join me on a committee that negotiates every year with Lord's. Through fair-minded co-operation from Lord's we've managed to achieve a formula that puts the umpire's contract on the same basic level as that of a county captain. We've also organized a pension scheme so that there's something there at the end of the day for an umpire who, after all, doesn't get a benefit or a testimonial like a player. The situation has also improved for umpires at

Test level. At the time when Packer turned cricket upside-down we were only getting £250 per Test. In the same season the England players' fee went up to £1,000 a time and we felt we should be getting nearer that for a job that needs concentration and skill at a high level. Within a couple of years we negotiated a satisfactory package, so that a decade after I got £75 for my first Test, we umpires now pick up over £1,000 each Test. That's bound to help the status of umpires because, as in every other walk of life, if you see good financial rewards available for the ones at the top of the tree, you try your hardest to reach that level.

Does cricket still have its appeal? In England, I think the answer is definitely, 'Yes'. Wherever I umpire, youngsters are always playing their impromptu games of cricket during the intervals (at places like Worcester and Southampton there are balls flying all over the place as the umpires walk back to the wicket), and the autograph hunters are still out in force. It's still a great game — if only because you can share your successes or disappointments. In golf, you can sink a 30-foot putt and be delighted with it yourself, yet nobody really wants to know about it in the clubhouse afterwards. But in cricket, if you take a great catch, if you bowl or bat beautifully, everybody keeps coming up and saying, 'Well done.' I believe that spirit of genuine sporting good fellowship is still prevalent in the English game, but there are one or two things I'd like to change.

I think wickets should be covered all the time in first-class cricket over here. It becomes a lottery if the toss determines the result; that can happen if it rains, so that the side batting first usually wins. I know it will take away a little bit of the glamour, because you won't be able to see any great defensive innings on sticky wickets, but the advantages are greater. It will mean that bowlers have to learn how to bowl people out, rather than just contain them or wait for the weather to play tricks. Most of the wickets in England are too slow; few batsmen consistently put their foot down the wicket and play through the line — they have to watch the ball on to the bat and work it away. So

104

techniques start deteriorating and our Test batsmen get into trouble when they play on fast, bouncy wickets abroad. Something must be done to make English wickets faster, otherwise we'll have no fast bowlers.

I'm concerned about slow over rates in Tests. I believe about 18 overs an hour should be bowled by all Test sides, otherwise the public is being short-changed. It's all very well to say that the spectators don't mind as long as they can see great fast bowling, but too often the fielding side dawdles around, just slowing down the game in a subtle manner, so that two batsmen who are well set have to take risks to get on with the game, simply because they aren't getting enough deliveries bowled at them. I get amused, and occasionally cross, when the fielding side suddenly wakes up to the fact that they can get another over in before the interval. That's when they rush around and look particularly keen. If I had my way they would lose that advantage, because I believe play should stop exactly at the appointed hour. If the intervals are scheduled for 1.30 and 4.15, and close of play is 6.30, I think the bails should come off when those times are reached. That would mean that two or three balls would be needed subsequently to complete the over, but so what? Nobody ever complains about the play being halted if a batsman is dismissed and the over is completed after the interval.

If anybody thinks that Test sides stacked with fast bowlers *can't* improve their bowling rates, take a look at the example shown by Mike Brearley's England side. Once fines for slow over rates were introduced, and it was made clear that the money would come from the players' pockets, they improved by two overs an hour. That's another 12 overs the spectator can see in a day. I believe that system should apply to all Test sides.

One other thing that's bothered me in the past has now been sorted out; a new way of being dismissed has been introduced to the laws of cricket — 'timed out'. In the past the fielding captain was powerless to stop the incoming batsman taking his time. This often happened if a nightwatchman was due in with just a few minutes of play left. I remember this happened in the Lord's Test of 1972 when Australia's Johnny Gleeson took three minutes to get to the crease after a wicket had fallen at 6.25. Ray Illingworth was getting annoyed because he suspected a spot of gamesmanship. We later found out the reason for Gleeson's delay — he got lost in the pavilion at Lord's and took the wrong turning. Under the new laws he could be given out — the fielding captain can appeal if the batsman takes longer than two minutes to step on to the field after the dismissal of the previous batsman. And if the new batsman still dawdles to the crease after stepping on to the field, it's up to the umpire to say, 'Come on, get moving.'

I'm a little worried about the rowdiness that's creeping into

*Crowd invasions are an increasing problem in modern cricket and there seems little that players and umpires can do about it. This was one of the worst invasions in recent years — at the Oval in 1976, when the West Indies captain Clive Lloyd's efforts to keep the crowd back from the wicket failed. Play was held up for eight minutes and the players had to leave the field*

106

some English crowds. It's something that none of us ever really experienced in this country until the mid-seventies and it's getting worse. It's nice to walk off the field in a leisurely way at the end of the day without being harassed, pushed and pummelled. A batsman who's scored an unbeaten century or a bowler who's done well deserves to savour the moment of joy and bask in the applause, because there are plenty of days when he doesn't do very well and just wants to slink away. Nowadays you have to sprint for the pavilion, and I'd like to see more police involved, if necessary, to keep the unruly minority at bay. On Sundays I'd close all the bars, despite the loss of takings. Some people go to a John Player match on a Sunday *not* to watch the cricket, but simply to have a booze-up because the bar is open all the time. Once they've got tanked up they

proceed to spoil the day for everyone else, with their moronic chants. If they realized they couldn't get any drink at the ground they'd stop coming, and the vast majority could sit back and enjoy the game.

But these are minor grouses in what is really a very pleasurable existence for me. I have an open-air job that's now well paid, I mix with people whose company I enjoy, and I have a secure winter job with a Bristol insurance company. From mid-July my wife and two daughters join me in our caravan as I umpire up and down the country, so I don't lose out on my family life. Looking back, I'm grateful to Leicestershire for closing one door so quickly — because that helped me push open another while I was still young.

# 9 Umpires and Scorers

If a game of cricket is going to be organized properly, it needs two competent, conscientious scorers as well as a couple of good umpires. The scorers are an extension of the chain of continuity that embodies a cricket match — the batsman scores runs, the bowler delivers the ball, the umpire supervises the whole process and the scorer records the events.

In first-class cricket we umpires work very closely with the scorers. I feel a little sorry for them sometimes, because they're often badgered by the press about certain aspects of the day's play. I think some of the press don't realize the amount of concentration needed in a scorer's job. After all, scorers are the official recorders of the game and have to concentrate on every ball and swing into a course of action before the next delivery. Around the counties there are some great characters in the scorers' box — at Northampton there's Jack Mercer, the old Glamorgan bowler who's a dab hand with the card tricks; at Edgbaston Charlie Grove; there's Ted Lester with Yorkshire; and Claude Lewis does the duties for Kent. A lot of county scorers are former first-class players and it's always interesting to have a natter with them about old times. They look after the umpires, as well. At the appropriate interval, they'll come up and say, 'Hey, there were a couple of five-ball overs in that session.' That kind of thing does happen, since it's only human nature that an umpire should miscount now and again. In

109

return, we'll do our best to clarify a dismissal on the field of play; if the ball's flicked the stumps and knocked off a bail and the wicket-keeper's standing up, the poor old scorer won't know whether the true dismissal is bowled, caught or stumped. What an umpire will do is make the action of a catch or take off a bail to give the scorer some idea of how the batsman was out.

One scorer per side is obviously preferable because it takes some of the pressure off the unlucky man and it will hopefully prevent errors. The scorers should use the same methods, although each one will probably have his own particular idiosyncrasies; but as long as they understand what each other is doing there should be no problems. Before someone starts scoring in a match, I think it's a good idea to sit in the scorers' box and just watch what's going on. A fair amount of responsibility is involved — a scorer has to be a neat writer and develop a habit of doing certain things automatically after each ball and at the end of each over. I think the aspiring umpire, too, should spend a few hours in the box before he ever stands in a match. In any event, the umpires should always meet the

PAGES 110–113 *The main signals a scorer must know — and remember to acknowledge*
BELOW *No ball*

ABOVE LEFT *Six*
ABOVE RIGHT
*New ball taken*

scorers before the game. A good place to meet is the scorers' box, because they can go over the method of posting the score and also discover if there are any likely problems in acknowledging the umpires' signals — for example if the sunshine is too dazzling. One thing an umpire likes is for the scorers to avoid any unnecessary interruption of play. It's better if the point to be clarified can be postponed until the fall of the next wicket or, if urgent, at the end of the over. Try at all times to keep the game moving.

The scorers must *never* assume that the umpire has failed to signal when he should have done, for example when the batsmen run and there is no signal. The scorers must credit the *striker* and not assume it was a bye. The scorers must record the umpire's decision even if they justifiably think it's a mistaken one — for example the scorers must enter in the book the actual

111

number of runs completed if no boundary is signalled, even though they could see that the ball had reached the boundary.

There are four areas in which the scorers can be inaccurate:

1. Lack of knowledge of the laws relating to scoring.

2. Failure by the umpire to keep the scorers informed on points about which there may be any doubt.

3. Bad signalling by the umpires, or failure by them to insist on their signals being acknowledged before allowing the game to continue.

4. Inaccurate entries and checking of totals by the scorers.

From that outline, it's obvious that the scorers must be competent enough to do certain things — they must check the scores frequently during the game, they must know what actually constitutes a run, and they must be able to recognize all the various umpires' signals. At the end of each over the

| MATCH BETWEEN | Gloucestershire and Surrey | | | | | |
|---|---|---|---|---|---|---|
| PLAYED AT | The Oval | ON Sat, Mon, Tues. 12th, 14th, 15th. June 1976 | | | | |
| UMPIRES | R. Julian & P. Rochford | SIDE WINNING TOSS Gloucestershire | | | | |
| SCORERS | A.G. Avery & J Hill | 1st INNINGS of Gloucestershire | | | | |

| ORDER | Time for 50/100 150/200 | Time IN OUT | BATSMEN | RUNS AS SCORED | HOW OUT | BOWLER | Totals |
|---|---|---|---|---|---|---|---|
| 1 | | 11.00 11.10 | Sadiq | 131 | ct Roope | Baker | 5. |
| 2 | 95 | 11.00 11.05 | Stovold R.W | 14141141141411244131111444224122 (77)4 / | bowled | Jackman | 81. |
| 3 | 92 154 11/21 179 305 | | Zaheer | 21121441411442444411111144 (100) 14144411211134121114414411111 41114114411442111112111 (148) 41414111411461111111114222111141 41111 | not Out | | 216. |
| 4 | | 4.10 4.11 | Procter M.J | 11 | bowled | Intikhab. | 2 |
| 5 | | 5.18 5.25 | Shephard D.R | 114242 / | ct Howarth | Jackman | 14 |
| 6 | | 6.00 6.14 | Foat J.C | | ct Younis | Intikhab. | 0. |
| 7 | | 5.15 5.50 | Brown A.S | 41111411141111112 (27) 4111114 | ct Roope | Baker | 39. |
| 8 | | 11.00 11.05 | Graveney D.A | 1 / | ct Skinner | Jackman | 1. |
| 9 | | 11.00 | Brassington A.J | 2111141 | not Out | | 11 |
| 10 | | | Davey J | | | | |
| 11 | | | Brain B.m | | | | |

REMARKS Lunch 13·15 153·1 (135 mins) 38 overs. Tea 16·15 296·5 (275 mins). 32 overs.
Overs completed 17·50 (350mins)

50· 95 mins 14·1 overs. 100 100 mins 27·1 overs. 150 132 mins 36·2 overs. 200 185 mins 54·4 overs.
250 234 mins 70+ overs. 300 276 mins. 82·1 overs. 350 316 mins 91·4 overs.

| B | + | 4 |
|---|---|---|
| L | 241132 | 13 |
| W | | 1 |
| NO | 111 | 3. |

| FALL OF WICKETS | 1 | 2 | 3 | 4 | 5 | 6 | 7 | 8 | 9 | 10 | TOTAL 390 · 7 wickets |
|---|---|---|---|---|---|---|---|---|---|---|---|
| | 15 | 171 | 178 | 221 | 224 | 343. | 344. | | | | (100 overs) |
| BATSMAN OUT | Sadiq | Stovold | Procter | Shephard | Foat | Brown. | Graveney | | | | Run Rate 65·00 |
| NOT OUT | Stovold | Zaheer | Zaheer | Zaheer | Zaheer | Zaheer | Zaheer | | | | Over Rate 17·85 |
| | | 74 | 79 | 106. | 109. | 183. | 193. | | | | |

Published & Printed by Wightman & Co., Ltd., 1/3 Brixton Road, S.W.9.

### LEFT AND FOLLOWING PAGES

*An example of the high quality that can be reached by a scorer with the necessary dedication, neatness and speed. It's the work of the Gloucestershire scorer Bert Avery, and it covers the county match against Surrey at the Oval in 1976. Note the information (left) on cumulative times for half centuries reached not only by the batsman but also for the team.*

| BOWLER | | 1 | 2 | 3 | 4 | 5 | 6 |
|---|---|---|---|---|---|---|---|
| Jackman. | R.D. | 1)<br>-.1.---<br>42)<br>2---1.--<br>60)<br>--.1.---<br>30)<br>-.321-1 | 3).<br>1. ---4--<br>42)<br>42 W----1<br>62)<br>63-.2.-W--<br>32)<br>85 --.1-2. | 5).<br>5 --.-14<br>44)<br>43 --.1---<br>64)<br>65 --.1.---<br>34)<br>88 4---11 | 7).<br>11. 1-.1---<br>46)<br>44 -.11---<br>66)<br>66 ----.-3<br>36)<br>94 11-1-- | 9)<br>13 (4)------<br>48)<br>46 ----31<br>68)<br>M --.-14-<br>38)<br>97 1.4--- | 11).<br>17 --.4---<br>50)<br>50 -4.----<br>70)<br>71 1.--11.<br>50)<br>102 -W---4 |
| Baker. | R.P. | 2)<br>-- 3--1.<br>36)<br>--2---<br>38)<br>1---1.1. | 4)<br>4 2-----<br>32)<br>43 -2.----<br>37)<br>81. --14-- | 6)<br>M Wx--2--<br>45 /--4-1.<br>36.1-20--- | 8)<br>6 --.11-2<br>75)<br>50 -.11422<br>87. | 10)<br>10 1.-4--<br>77)<br>60 -.104-- | 12).<br>15 --.1---<br>75)<br>66 ----.-0 |
| Roope. | G.R.J. | 13).<br>-----1 | 15)<br>1 4.--11. | 17)<br>7 -1----- | 19)<br>8 ---.-1-- | 21)<br>9 --.1--4. | 23).<br>13 4.4--- |
| Butcher. | A.R. | | 24)<br>--3-2-- | 26)<br>5 --.1--- | 28)<br>6. 1-.444 19/ | | |
| Intikhab Alam. | | 29)<br>4.4----<br>48)<br>--.-4--<br>68)<br>----.11 | 31)<br>8 ----1--<br>51)<br>39 4.---4<br>71)<br>65 4.111-4 | 33).<br>9 ---.-1.<br>55)<br>M --5.-5.<br>73)<br>76 4.1-.4. | 35)<br>M ----4<br>55)<br>M --.2-1.<br>72)<br>85 141-.-- | 37)<br>13 -4.----<br>57)<br>42 ---.-1-<br>87)<br>91. 4111461 | 39)<br>17 1.-4.<br>59)<br>43 --.4---<br>103/ |

Surrey. BOWLING ANALY[SIS]

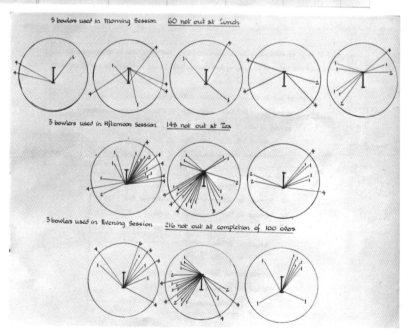

**ABOVE AND OPPOSITE ABOVE**
*The Surrey bowling analysis. In the top left-hand corner of each section you can see which over of the innings it was, and on the bottom right-hand corner of every over you can tell at a glance how many runs have come off that particular bowler in the entire innings. The circles round various deliveries denote no-balls. The W sign means a wicket was taken, and M signifies a maiden over*

5 bowlers used in morning Session.   60 not out at Lunch

3 bowlers used in Afternoon Session.   148 not out at Tea

3 bowlers used in Evening Session.   216 not out at completion of 100 overs

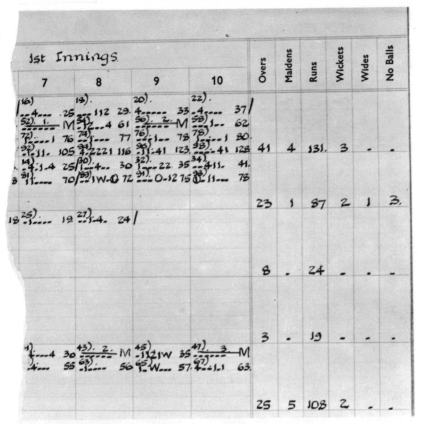

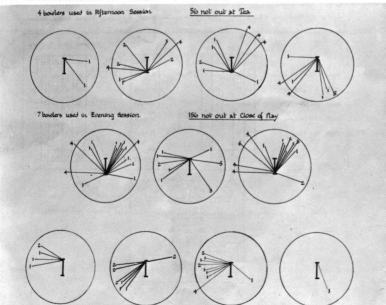

OPPOSITE BELOW AND LEFT *Bert Avery's scoring charts for the two centuries scored by Zaheer Abbas in that match. Heaven knows how Bert manages to grab the time to compile them while attending to the more mundane duties of keeping score — but they're a fascinating study of where a batsman scores his runs. As you can see, Zaheer is particularly strong on the off side*

scorers must agree about the number of runs in that over, the total number of runs in the innings up to that time, and the total of runs scored off the bowler who's just finished his over. On the fall of a wicket they must agree on the runs scored by the dismissed batsman and on the amount of runs and extras scored by the batting side. All common sense, I suppose, but they *are* important checks. But the vital part of the relationship between scorers and umpires concerns the signals — the umpire must always signal clearly to the box, and he mustn't allow the game to continue till his signal is acknowledged. If you want to signal a leg-bye and you just tap your leg with your hand, the scorers might not see that clearly from a distance of 90 yards. The umpire should stand aside from the fielders and make a clear, precise signal, accompanied if necessary by a call to the scorers.

# 10 A Quiz for Umpires

I know how many players like to try to catch an umpire out on a technicality, and I know from my own personal experience how many club cricket umpires pride themselves on their knowledge of the laws. Try these 20 questions. The answers are on the next page.

## QUESTIONS

1. If a bowler changes from bowling over to around the wicket without informing the umpire, what decision will the umpire give?

2. What circumstances decide which batsman is run out, when they are both attempting to run?

3. If the umpire sees that the batsman is out, but no appeal is made, what decision will he give?

4. When does the ball become dead?

5. An umpire calls 'No ball' but the ball does not leave the bowler's hand. What should he do?

6. The ball comes to rest in front of the striker's wicket and the umpire considers it to have been delivered. A fieldsman then interferes with the ball. What action should the umpire take?

7. The striker is hit on the leg by the bowler with the ball and, in pain, hits it hard back up the wicket. On appeal what decision would you give?

117

8. Both batsmen at the wicket leave the field, or the fieldsmen at any time without agreement of the umpires leave the field. Can the match be awarded to the other side on appeal?

9. How many reasons can you think of to allow either umpire to call 'dead ball'?

10. What constitutes a wide?

11. If an umpire miscounts the number of balls in an over, what happens?

12. What is the latest time captains should toss before the game starts?

13. How many ways can you be out from a wide?

14. What penalty is incurred if the fieldsman stops the ball other than with a part of his person?

15. Name the ten ways of being dismissed.

16. If the non-striker obstructs a fieldsman from making a catch, which batsman is out?

17. What is the only Test-playing country not to have had an umpire officiate on the first-class list?

18. The batsman plays the ball in the air on to the stumps at the far end. The bowler just touches it with the batsman out of his ground and the ball is then caught by mid-off. How is the batsman out and why?

19. What is the only position in which a captain may object to a substitute fielding?

20. If the ball is stationary and then a batsman accidentally kicks a ball on to his wicket and breaks it, what is the correct decision?


## ANSWERS

1. Call 'No ball'. (Law 24.1)

2. If the batsmen have crossed in running, the man who runs for the wicket which is broken is out. If they have *not* crossed, the one who has left the wicket which has been broken is out. (Law 38.1)

3. The umpire shall *not* give a batsman out unless appealed to by the other side. (Law 27.1)

4. When:

(a) It is finally settled in the hands of the wicket-keeper or bowler.

(b) It reaches or pitches over the boundary.

(c) A batsman is out.

(d) Whether played or not, if it lodges in the clothing or equipment of a batsman or the clothing of an umpire.

(e) A ball lodges in a protective helmet worn by a member of the fielding side.

(f) A penalty is awarded under Law 20 (lost ball) or Law 41.1 (fielding the ball).

(g) The umpire calls 'Over' or 'Time'. (Law 23.1)

5. Revoke the call. (Law 24.7)

6. The umpire shall replace the ball where it came to rest and shall order the fieldsmen to resume the places they occupied in the field before the ball was delivered. (Law 25.3)

7. 'Out'. Hit the ball twice. (Law 34)

8. Yes. (Law 21.3)

9. (a) He intervenes in a case of unfair play.

(b) A serious injury occurs to a player or umpire.

(c) He is satisfied that, for an adequate reason, the striker is not ready to receive the ball and makes no attempt to play it.

(d) The bowler drops the ball accidentally before delivery, or the ball does not leave his hand for any reason.

(e) One or both bails fall from the striker's wicket before he is ready for the delivery.

(f) He leaves his normal position for consultation.

(g) He is required to do so under Law 26.3, i.e. disallowing of leg-byes etc.

(Law 23.2)

10. If the bowler bowls a ball so high over *or* so wide of the wicket that, in the opinion of the umpire, it passes out of reach of the striker who is standing in his normal position. The

119

umpire must call and signal 'Wide ball' as soon as it has passed the line of the striker's wicket. (Law 25.1)

11. The over as counted by the umpire stands. (Law 22.4)

12. 15 minutes. (Law 12.3)

13. Five — hit wicket, stumped, run out, handled ball, obstructing the field. (Law 25.7)

14. Five runs shall be added to the run or runs already scored. If no run has been scored, 5 penalty runs shall be allowed. (Law 41.1)

15. (a) Bowled.

    (b) Caught.

    (c) Run out.

    (d) Stumped.

    (e) Handled the ball.

    (f) Hit ball twice.

    (g) Lbw.

    (h) Hit wicket.

    (i) Obstructing the field.

    (j) Timed out.

16. Striker. (Law 37)

17. Pakistan.

18. Bowler credited with wicket (caught). (Law 32)

19. Wicket-keeper. (Law 2.2)

20. Not out (Law 30)